A Brief History of Citizenship

Derek Heater

NEW YORK UNIVERSITY PRESS
Washington Square, New York

First published in the U.S.A. in 2004 by
NEW YORK UNIVERSITY PRESS
Washington Square
New York, NY 10003
www.nyupress.org

First published in Great Britain in 2004 by
Edinburgh University Press
22 George Square
Edinburgh

© Derek Heater, 2004

A Cataloging-in-Publication Data record for this book is
available from the Library of Congress.

ISBN 0-8147-3671-8 (cloth : alk. paper)
ISBN 0-8147-3672-6 (paper : alk. paper)

Typeset in 10/12 Times New Roman
by Simon Kear, and
printed and bound in Great Britain by
MPG Books Ltd, Bodmin, Cornwall

Contents

Preface

Citizenship became a topic of keen interest throughout the world in three spheres during the 1990s: socio-political, academic and educational. This interest has generated an immense literature; yet there does not exist, to my knowledge, any single book that surveys the whole history of the principles and practice of citizenship throughout its entire span. However, the current conditions and debates cannot be fully understood without a knowledge of the historical background; indeed, a great deal of the literature on the subject justifies itself by allusions to past theories and practices. This book seeks to provide the essential historical material through an analytical narrative from Sparta to the present day, *c*.700 BC to AD 2000, including quotations from key texts.

Few writers emerge from their work without incurring debts of gratitude. My first thanks, as ever, must be recorded to my wife for her unstinting help. Other thank-yous are to my friends, Professor G.R. Berridge and Simon Kear. They both encouraged me to write this book and Simon produced it originally as an ebook and provided the technical skill of preparing a useable disk. Finally, I am grateful to Nicola Carr and her colleagues for their faith that this is a worthwhile project.

Derek Heater
Rottingdean, 2003

Introduction

Socio-political identities

Citizenship is a form of socio-political identity. But it is only one of several, with which it has co-existed at various times during the two-and-three-quarter millennia of its life to date. Sometimes it has lived in harmony with other forms, sometimes in competition; sometimes it has been the dominant form of identity, sometimes it has been submerged by others; sometimes it has been distinct from other kinds, sometimes subsumed into one or another.

We may discern five main forms of identity which human beings can experience in their capacity as socio-political animals: they are found in the feudal, monarchical, tyrannical, national and citizenship systems respectively. Each of these is rooted in a basic relationship, and each involves the individual in having a status, a feeling about the relationship, and competence to behave appropriately in that context. Apart from the willingness and competence to fight on behalf of the system, which is common to all these identities, we can recognize important differences between them.

A feudal relationship was hierarchical, status determined by the bonds between vassal or man and lord. The feeling that the individual has in this system was formed by the reciprocal nature of the relationship – service by him below, protection by him above: a simple pyramidal pattern. Consequently, the competence required was dependent upon the individual's station in life.

In a monarchical system the monarch – the single ruler – is set apart from all other inhabitants of the polity, who have the status of his or her subjects. The subjects are expected to display the feeling of loyalty to the Crown and person of the monarch as a personification of the country. The competence expected of the subject is minimal because what is essentially required is passive obedience.

Tyranny, by which we mean all forms of authoritarian government including dictatorship and modern totalitarianism, is a distorted version of one-person rule. The status of the individual is further degraded to the all-consuming purpose of supporting the tyrant's regime. Political feeling is an activated love of the person of the tyrant. And the only competence needed is that of involvement in the mobilized support for the tyrant.

When individuals identify with the nation they are recognizing their status as members of a cultural group (however defined). The feeling associated with this form of identity is love of the nation and a consciousness of its traditions. Therefore, knowledge of what has made and still makes the nation 'great' is a required kind of competence.

And so we come to citizenship. This defines the relationship of the individual not to another individual (as is the case with the feudal, monarchical and tyrannical systems) or a group (as with nationhood), but essentially to the idea of the state. The civic identity is enshrined in the rights conveyed by the state and the duties performed by the individual citizens, who are all autonomous persons, equal in status. Good citizens are those who feel an allegiance to the state and have a sense of responsibility in discharging their duties. As a consequence they need the skills appropriate for this civic participation.

The notions of autonomy, equality of status and citizenly participation in the affairs of the polity set citizenship theoretically apart from the feudal, monarchical and tyrannical forms of socio-political identity. The hierarchical structure of feudalism and the expectations of submissiveness of all these other three styles would seem to render them incompatible with citizenship properly speaking. In the case of feudalism, citizenship may indeed be interpreted as emancipation from the bound status, as indicated in Chapter Three. Even so, citizenship in some form – arguably in weak or disfigured forms – has been associated with both monarchical

Table Intro 1. Distinctions between socio-political identities

System	Land	Person	Concept
Feudal	basis of relationship	reciprocal bonds	
Monarchical		loyalty	
Tyrannical		focus of system	religion/ ideology
Nation	territory of nation		idealization
Citizenship			states/rights duties

and tyrannical modes of government, as will be revealed in Chapters Three and Six.

The identity that has become especially closely associated with citizenship is nationhood. Indeed, from c.1800 to c.2000 they became for all intents and purposes fused as the idea took hold that the state and nation should be coterminous. This is an issue that will occupy our attention in Chapter Five.

Another way of interpreting the distinctions just outlined is to notice the patterns that can be made by juxtaposing attachment to a person, attachment to land and attachment to an abstract concept (see *Table Intro 1*).

Models of the history of citizenship

These high levels of generalization must not be allowed to give the impression that all is that simple. Citizenship is certainly not simple in either theory or practice. Indeed, attempts at explaining this form of identity have produced many different models of both its essence and its historical development. A brief survey of a few of these historical interpretations will show how each illuminates our subject.

Some scholars have discerned patterns by concentrating on a limited selection of material. Most famous and influential of these is T.H. Marshall's *Citizenship and Social Class.* In these lectures, delivered in 1949, he identified three forms of citizenship, namely civil (e.g. equality before the law), political (e.g. the vote) and social (e.g. welfare state), which, he argued, developed historically in that order. The detail of his analysis has been subjected to some criticism, mainly because he drew his data only from the experience of English men. Despite consequent reservations about generalizing from the limited purpose of Marshall's lectures, the basic notion of a tripartite content of citizenship rights has remained useful. Accordingly, we shall be examining this interpretation in Chapter Six.

More recently, J.G.A. Pocock has posited a dual strain in the history of citizenship from classical times. For the Greeks, notably Aristotle, being a citizen was natural: a man was *zoon politikon*, a political animal. For the Romans, in contrast, man was a legal entity; as a citizen, he had a legal relationship with the state:

> The advent of jurisprudence moved the concept of the 'citizen' from the *zoon politikon* towards the *legalis homo*, and from the *civis* or *polites* [the Latin and Greek for 'citizen' respectively] toward the

bourgeois or *burger*. It further brought about some equation of the 'citizen' with the 'subject', for in defining him as the member of a community of law, it emphasized that he was, in more senses than one, the subject of those laws that defined his community and of the rulers and magistrates empowered to enforce them.   (Pocock, 1995, p. 38)

Peter Riesenberg, in his *Citizenship in the Western Tradition: Plato to Rousseau*, offers two patterns for the reader's consideration, very different from Pocock's. His core thesis is that there have been two phases in the history of citizenship, with a transition period of roughly a hundred years from the late eighteenth century. The 'first citizenship' was characterized by an

intimate world [of small-scale societies] and the forces that held it together... when most historically and morally conscious people lived in such communities and had remarkably similar ideas about what a good person's conduct should be and how to develop it, generation after generation.   (Riesenberg, 1992, p. xv)

The pivot which swung the western world into the 'second citizenship' was the age of the late eighteenth-century revolutions. The old elitist citizenship of virtue was gradually displaced by a more inclusive, democratic, national citizenship, centred on the requirement of loyalty.

Riesenberg's other insight is the fluctuating nature of the first citizenship as commitment to the ideal waxed and waned, or, as he expresses it, a succession of 'perfect moments' followed by decline: 'the age of Solon, the early Roman Republic, the first days of the medieval commune, perhaps even the birth years of the American Republic. In such moments citizenship may really have worked' (Reisenberg, 1992, p. xxiii).

Whereas Riesenberg sees a pattern of first and second citizenships, most other students of the subject describe a slightly different duality, namely a distinction between what are usually termed the 'civic republican' and 'liberal' traditions.

The civic republican (or 'classical' or 'civic humanist') kind of thinking about citizenship has argued that the best form of state is based on two supports. These are: a citizenry of politically virtuous men; and a just mode of government – the state must be a 'republic' in the sense of a constitutionally governed polity, not one governed arbitrarily, not a tyranny. Both elements – good civic behaviour and a republican form of state – were essential, hence the term 'civic republican'. A community of free citizens was impossible under a tyranny; a 'republic' was impossible without the active support and participation of citizens. Citizenship therefore entailed primarily duty and civic virtue. We shall come across these ideas particularly in the surveys of Aristotle, Machiavelli and Rousseau.

The alternative, liberal view evolved in the seventeenth and eighteenth centuries and became by far the stronger in the nineteenth and twentieth. This school of thought argues that the state exists for the benefit of its citizens, has an obligation, indeed, to ensure that they have and enjoy certain rights. Using Marshall's triad, we should note that, when seventeenth- and eighteenth-century writers and politicians referred to rights, they meant civil and political rights, though social rights did make a tentative early appearance in the French Revolution.

Our purpose in outlining these interpretations is not to judge or challenge or replace them, but merely to show that different patterns can and have been discerned by scholars in this field. In the chapters that follow none of these models, nor any other, shapes the presentation. Readers are offered a simple narrative – for its own sake, or as a means of fleshing out the interpretations just outlined, as they wish.

CHAPTER ONE

Greece

Sparta

Origins

Our story may be conveniently started in a cluster of four little Greek villages in the south of the Peloponnese peninsula. The date is very approximately 700 BC; the evidence is too shadowy for us to be more precise. These villages, which collectively at about this date formed the *polis* – the city-state – of Sparta, were settlements in the fertile plain of Laconia, or Lacedaemon. Hence, their inhabitants are referred to alternatively as 'Spartans' or 'Lacedaemonians'. And, because of the disciplined mode of discourse which the elite class was educated to perfect, their manner of speech has given the English language the word 'laconic', as well as the word 'spartan', the latter derived from their austere style of living.

Sparta might, indeed, well appear a strange originator of the idea of citizenship, which we today essentially associate with the notion and practice of beneficial liberal rights and extended political discussion. After all, from a modern perspective, the accepted image of Sparta is most unprepossessing. One British scholar has characterized it as 'A militaristic and totalitarian state, holding down an enslaved population, the helots, by terror and violence, educating its young by a system incorporating all the worst features of the traditional English public school, and deliberately turning its back on the intellectual and artistic life of the rest of Greece' (quoted, Plutarch, 1988, p. ix).

Yet, to start the reader on the historical journey of citizenship in Sparta is not an eccentric whim or paradox. We must keep in mind three considerations. One is that we have little knowledge of any earlier form of participative political society from which we can trace a continuous narrative of the principle and practice of citizenship. Secondly, by no means all political thinkers and commentators, from ancient Greece down to the present, have harboured darkly negative feelings about the

Spartan system. And thirdly, history as evolution is, of course, just that
– a process of change and adaptation from the starting-point. So, then,
what happened in Sparta that brought about the firming up for a cadre of
its inhabitants of a status we can genuinely recognise as and justifiably
call citizenship?

From their four villages the Spartans gradually expanded, annexing
their neighbours' lands to the east. To the west, in the opposite direction,
stand the Taygetus Mountains. In the late eighth century BC the Spartans
ventured across these heights and, in a fiercely contested conflict,
worsted the inhabitants of that region, the Messenians, conquered their
land and subjugated them to a condition akin to slavery. They became
helots, a form of subjection which was then transmitted throughout all
the Spartans' territories and became consolidated as the defining socio-
economic basis of their life. However, the Messenians did not respond
meekly to their loss of freedom. A military elite of select Spartans was
accordingly necessary to impose stable control. It was this elite – called
'Spartiates' – who had the identifiable status of citizens. The emergence
of this citizenly class in these circumstances poses two important
questions: How did their status originate? What criteria were established
that distinguished them as citizens?

Firmly embedded in Greek tradition was the belief that a great
law-giver named Lycurgus framed a body of constitutional, social
and economic reforms in the early eighth century BC. Among other
provisions, Lycurgus is credited with formalizing the class of privileged
and dutiful citizens which was in all probability already in ill-defined
existence. A full and lucid account of Lycurgus' measures has come
down to us in a biographical sketch written some eight hundred years
later by the great biographer and writer on moral principles, Plutarch.
The trouble is, modern historians are not at all sure whether a man called
Lycurgus actually existed (there is even a hint that the Greeks thought
him to have been a god); or whether the reforms attributed to him were
the work of one person at one given time (see Talbert in Plutarch, 1988,
pp. 1–3). The reader might therefore like to think of inverted commas
placed round the name.

The facets of Spartan citizenship

These reforms produced a citizenly style with a number of interlocking
facets, all essential for the Spartiate mode of citizenship. These were: the
principle of equality; ownership of a portion of public land; economic
reliance on the work of the helots; a rigorous regime of upbringing and
training; the taking of meals in common messes; military service; the

attribute of civic virtue; and participation in the government of the state. A formidable list, so let us expand on each feature in turn.

The Spartiates themselves – perhaps some 9,000 in the Lycurgan age – referred to each other as *Homoioi*, which may be rendered as 'Equals' or 'Peers'. Since they were a privileged elite, the aristocratic overtone of the English word 'peer' is a fitting translation. Equality has always been a slippery concept; and it is not absolutely clear what it connoted in ancient Sparta. The prolific Greek writer Xenophon explained in *c.*400 BC that Lycurgus 'gave an equal share in the state to all law-abiding citizens, without regard for physical or financial deficiencies' (Plutarch, 1988, p. 177). The Peers were unlikely to have been equal in wealth, though several commentaries suggest that they were. What the Lycurgan reforms probably did enact was a redistribution of parcels of public lands (*kleroi*) to the Spartiates so that each had at least a minimum floor of income from agricultural produce. Ownership of a *kleros* was therefore the second feature of the Spartiate status.

However, the citizens did not farm their lands themselves: this was the task of the helots, who, under threat of capital punishment for non-compliance, were required to hand over the produce they garnered from the land they worked. Indeed, citizenship and manual work, even the pursuit of a craft, were, generally speaking, reckoned mutually incompatible. As Aristotle observed, the Spartiates wore their hair long as a style precluding a life of labour. To put the matter bluntly, the Spartan citizenry were economically utterly dependent on slave labour; the whole Lycurgan concept of citizenship was founded on this system.

What, then, did the Spartiates in fact do? They defended and governed the state. As a preparation for these functions – in particular their military service – novice Spartiates underwent an extraordinarily strict and severe programme of training (*agogē*). (Spartiate offspring who were obvious weaklings and who would therefore not grow to a condition able to endure this regime were exposed so that they would die.) At seven years of age each boy was allocated to a group of companions with whom he lived and trained until he was twenty. The curriculum (if we may use the term for an upbringing that so lightly touched on education as we understand it) was designed to develop feats of endurance to the limits of human physique and will-power. This objective was attained by fierce discipline. During their twenties the young men were quasi-citizens, with military duties but without civic rights and responsibilities. Some of these young men, serving under an adult chief trainer, were placed in charge of the boys for the purpose of leading them and instilling the demanded attitudes and behaviour. The specified pedagogical method was the liberal use of the whip, even flogging to death, no doubt *pour encourager les autres.*

A story which has come down the ages concerns a Fagin–like induction. The boys were taught to steal as a means of developing initiative, cunning and practice in evasion. Theft was not a crime; being caught was. The anecdote, as related by Plutarch, runs as follows: '[a boy] had stolen a fox cub and had it concealed inside his cloak: in order to escape detection he was prepared to have his insides clawed and bitten out by the animal, and even to die' (Plutarch, 1988, p. 30). Apocryphal or true, Plutarch believed it a credible illustration of the Spartan mode of training for citizenship.

Another gruesome feature of these preparatory years was a kind of commando training called *krypteia.* Plutarch's account is again illuminating:

> Periodically the overseers of the young men would dispatch into the countryside in different directions the ones who appeared to be particularly intelligent; they were equipped with daggers and basic rations, but nothing else. By the day they would disperse to obscure spots in order to hide and rest. At night they made their way to roads and murdered any helot whom they caught. Frequently, too, they made their way through fields, killing the helots who stood out for their physique and strength.   (Plutarch, 1988, pp. 40–1)

This last sentence reveals the secondary purpose of these expeditions: to cull from the helot population any who might be dangerous rebels capable of threatening Spartiate control.

When the young man was ready to be incorporated into the body of citizens, he had to be elected to a mess (which will be explained below) and be able to pay his 'mess dues', which he could meet from his *kleros.* Both election and payment of dues were crucial for becoming and remaining a citizen. Plutarch once more provides us with a vivid description of the election process:

> Each member would take a piece of soft bread in his hand and in silence would throw it, like a ballot, into the bowl which a servant carried on his head. Those in favour threw the bread as it was, while those against squeezed it hard with their hand. The effect of a squeezed piece is that of a hollow ballot. And should they find even one of these, they do not admit the would-be entrant because it is their wish that all should be happy in each other's company. (Plutarch, 1988, p. 21)

And that was it – no second chance, no application to an alternative mess. Nor was a successful candidate's membership permanently secure. If he ever failed to pay his mess dues, he would be expelled and, as a consequence, lose his status as a citizen.

We need, therefore, to explain briefly this system of messes, which the Spartans called *phiditia*. Each mess was composed of perhaps about 300 members (we are not at all sure), who were required to take their meals there, and not at home. Every month they paid their dues in specified amounts of barley-meal, cheese, figs, wine and a small sum of money. The purpose of this institution of communal eating was to keep firm the sense of camaraderie ingrained in the Spartiate class in their period of training. As Plutarch says of Lycurgus: 'Altogether he accustomed citizens to have no desire for a private life, nor knowledge of one, but rather be like bees, always attached to the community, swarming together around their leader, and almost ecstatic with fervent ambition to devote themselves entirely to their country' (Plutarch, 1988, p. 37). It goes without saying that Sparta has not been the only state to use training for and service in the army as the surest method of building and sustaining an *esprit de corps*.

One of the most famous heroic exploits in military history was the self-sacrificial stand made at Thermopylae against Xerxes' huge Persian force by Leonidas and his 300 crack Spartiate troops. The tactical excellence of Greek armies was founded on their contingents of heavily-armed infantry, called 'hoplites'. In the Sparta of Lycurgan times a hoplite was a citizen and a citizen (of active age) was a hoplite. Spartiates were consequently required to involve themselves in persistent training in order to keep their bodies in peak condition and their fighting skills honed to perfection. Hence their reliance on the labour of their helots and the productive work of non-slave inhabitants of Laconia: as specialist warriors, though generously provided with leisure, they had no time to be farmers as well.

Good soldiers, as the Spartiates undoubtedly were, must be possessed of unwavering courage. They must also be steadfastly loyal and deeply committed to duty. These characteristics are embraced in the Greek word *arete*, which may, albeit inadequately, be translated as 'civic virtue' or 'excellence' or 'goodness'. (A fuller explanation of the concept appears in the next section of this chapter.)

Tyrtaeus, who wrote in the seventh century BC, was a kind of poet laureate for Sparta; and from the surviving fragments of his work we can glimpse the Spartan ideal man, possessed of this *aretē*. In military terms he paints a word-portrait of the soldier risking his life for his city. This was the new citizenly frame of mind, in sharp contrast to the heroes of Homer, who fought valiantly for their personal glory. In the stilted translation we have, Tyrtaeus declared that, 'a common good this, both for the city and all her people, when a man standeth firm in the forefront without ceasing, and making heart and soul to abide. . . moreover, he that falleth in the van and loseth life to the glory of his city and countrymen [is]. . . lamented with sore regret by all the city' (Edmonds, 1961, p. 75).

Civilian duty conscientiously performed was also expected of the good citizen. This would involve virtuous obedience to the laws and participation in the Assembly. What is stressed by authorities such as Xenophon and Plutarch is the penalty of loss of citizenship for any man whose behaviour fell short of these expectations. Thus Xenophon: 'Lycurgus made it clear that if anyone should shirk the effort required to keep his laws, then he would no longer be considered one of the Equals' (Plutarch, 1988, p. 177). Cowardice was even worse: moral weakness on the battlefield was not only punished by the derogation of the Spartiate's citizenly status, but there ensued a wide range of social expressions of scorn for his ignominious conduct. Cowards were despised as 'tremblers'.

However, and finally in our list of the criteria for Spartan citizenship, we come to participation in the processes of government, the political element of citizenship that has been so central to the modern concept of the status. The Lycurgan constitution reduced the power of the kings (Sparta had two reigning simultaneously) by providing for an Assembly and a tiny Senate or Council of Elders (*Gerousia*). The latter comprised the kings, and 28 elders, aged at least 60, elected by the Assembly, itself composed of Spartiates aged at least 30. All citizens were therefore able to participate, though there is some scholarly dispute concerning the relative powers of the Assembly and the Council of Elders.

The system probably worked something like this. The Council of Elders was the supreme political and judicial body. In terms of making policy and laws it was this institution which had the authority to initiate proposals. These were laid before the regular meetings of the Assembly, which had the power of decision-making – unless, that is, in the words of an ancient text, the Assembly 'speaks crookedly' (see Cartledge, 1979, p. 135). In such circumstances the elders and kings had the power to override the Assembly. The Lycurgan reforms can be construed as a replacement of government by a dyarchy with a balanced constitution of government by citizens. The generality of the Spartiates acted through an Assembly with decision-making powers and powers of amendment, while a handful of the most experienced drafted legislation and blocked any unwise counter-proposals from the 'lower house': Plutarch calls the elders 'a kind of ballast' (Plutarch, 1988, p. 13).

Problems with Spartan citizenship

Certainly stability was, by received tradition, Lycurgus' prime objective. The Greek word is *eunomia*, good order, for the community and the state, socially as well as politically. But no society or state can remain static. In due course, the gap between the wealthy and poorer Spartiates widened: the 'Equals' no longer even approximated to equality. The poorer were unable to pay their mess dues and were therefore demoted from their status. For this and other reasons, such as refusal to recruit into the Spartiate caste from social inferiors or high-class foreign families, the number of Spartiates steadily declined. Three historians give us telling figures: Herodotus – 8,000 in 480 BC; Thucydides – 3,500 in 418; and Xenophon – 1,500 in 371.

On the other hand, the hoplite force had to be kept up to strength. So the Lycurgan precepts of Spartiate caste excellence were perforce relaxed. Non-Spartiates were recruited; and there is even evidence of cowardice being exonerated to prevent derogation. The equations of citizen and hoplite, and citizenship and the virtue of fortitude, lauded in Tyrtaeus' elegiac poems and famed throughout Greece, could not be sustained.

And yet, this dilution of the Spartan style of citizenship was not the only problem. There were, in addition, intrinsic faults in the system. The rank of citizen was a highly privileged status, based upon and sustained by the exploitation of the helot underclass. By humane standards the *agoge* was savage, and the stress on military training and service as the primary distinctive feature of citizenship was a distortion of what the civic status should entail: Lycurgan citizenship was a lop-sided interpretation of the concept. Aristotle was convinced of this. He declared: 'The whole system of legislation is directed to fostering only one part or element of goodness – goodness in war. . . . The Spartans. . . did not know how to use the leisure which peace brought; and they never accustomed themselves to any discipline other than that of war' (Aristotle, 1948, 1271b). At root, indeed, the Spartiate mode of citizenship was artificial and strained. For example, Plutarch tells us that, for fear that the imposed standards would be tainted and weakened, Lycurgus 'did not grant Spartiates permission to be away from the city and to travel freely, acquiring foreign habits and copying lifestyles based upon no training as well as types of government different from that of Sparta' (Plutarch, 1988, p. 40).

On the other hand, the Lycurgan constitution did establish what became perennial principles of citizenship, even if they were subsequently often achieved only rather roughly in practice. Citizens should exist in conditions of basic equality with each other; they should have a keen sense of civic duty; they should participate in the political affairs of their state; and they should be ready to defend their country. Partly because these have been considered down the ages to be admirable qualities, and partly because the people of Sparta, one way or another, paid a heavy price for their development, the Spartiate form of citizenship has afforded constant fascination.

Figure 1.1. The Spartiate System

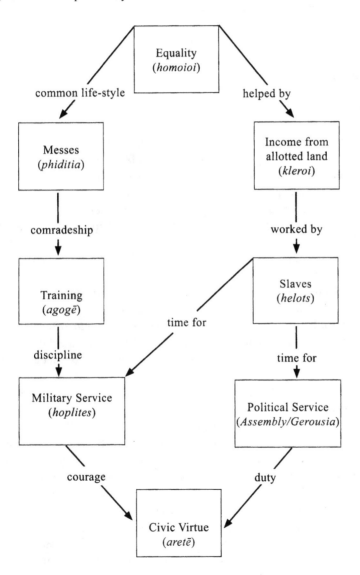

However, because Sparta prized military endeavour at the expense of scholarly enquiry, the Lacedaemonians produced no political theorist who might have supplied us with enlightening commentary. Political theory and analysis was born in Athens, and its two most distinguished exponents, Plato and his pupil Aristotle, made careful studies in the fourth century BC of the Spartan constitution and way of life, though their judgments were coloured by their own beliefs about the qualities and functions which should desirably characterize the condition of citizenship.

Plato and Aristotle

Plato

Plato was born in 428 BC and lived to the ripe old age of about 81, dying in 347. Both his father's and mother's families had landed wealth. However, influenced by the troubles Athens was undergoing during his lifetime and perhaps by his attachment to Socrates, some forty years his senior, he decided to pursue a life of philosophical enquiry and teaching rather than public service. For his educational purpose he founded the Academy; and for a wider audience he produced his dialogues, three of which are devoted to politics – the *Republic*, the *Laws* and the less important *Statesman*.

To Plato's mind – and he shared these views with many other aristocratic Athenians – the Spartan system had much to commend it. Not, in truth, its brutality (he considered the *krypteia* offensive), but its stability and orderliness. He also admired the Spartiates' disciplined and austere life-style and their willing devotion to the ultimate point of offering their very lives for their city's preservation. Plato even approved the division of labour whereby the top echelons of citizens undertook no manual work. How clearly one can hear the echo of Lycurgan Sparta in Plato's *Republic*. In this ideal state: 'Authority will be respected; the fighting class will abstain from any form of business, farming, or handicrafts; they will keep up their common meals and give their time to physical training and martial exercises' (Plato, 1941, VIII. 546). Except that in Plato's state the citizenry are divided into three classes. These are the Guardians, who govern; the soldiers, who defend (to whom the above extract refers); and the producers. This last and, naturally, largest component embraces all professional, business and working men; and although (unlike the Spartan system) they are citizens, they are very much second-class, passive citizens, not expected, it seems, to participate in public affairs.

The state that emerges from the *Republic* is Plato's unattainable vision of perfection. He sketched a more realistic model in the *Laws*. The size of his proposed *polis* (city-state) in this work is quite precise, namely, 5,040 citizen households. Here, as in Sparta, all the citizens are relieved of or precluded from economically productive labour. A class of serfs cultivate the land, while business and industry are in the hands of non-citizen resident aliens. The status of citizenship is inherited through both lines of descent. However, unlike the Lycurgan arrangements, Plato's hypothetical citizens are not equal, they are divided into four classes or grades according to their computed wealth. Moreover, this device has highly significant political implications via the electoral system.

Plato provides for a representative Council, a quarter of whose membership is chosen by each of the citizen classes. Consequently, on the assumption that the number of citizens in each class is inversely related to the wealth of each class, the richest would be proportionately more generously represented than the poorest. Further undemocratic provisions are the exaction of penalties for non-voting from only the wealthy and the restriction of certain offices to the top classes. Thus the poorer citizens have both weak inducements and limited opportunities to participate in the political affairs of their state.

Plato's prime objective is a stable and harmonious polity. He wants friendly and trusting relationships between citizens, whose social bonding is achieved, at least in part, through the institution of Spartiate-style messes. Good citizens are those who are deferent to the social and political system, are law-abiding, and who exercise self-control.

These qualities are fostered by the state-run schools. Plato, it should be remembered, is as distinguished a philosopher of education as a philosopher of politics: the *Republic* in particular has much to say on what he believed to be ideal pedagogy. In the *Laws* he provides a succinct statement: 'What we have in mind is education in virtue, a training which produces a keen desire to become a perfect citizen who knows how to rule and be ruled as justice demands' (Plato, 1970, I. 643). Collaborative activities such as dance, acting and athletics produce considerate, cooperative citizens. And public festivals are so designed as to continue this socially educative process throughout life. In contradistinction to Sparta, however, the virtues which Plato wished to cultivate were those necessary for civil concord, not the successful prosecution of war.

Aristotle on citizenship

Plato did not just theorise about education; he was a teacher, and his most distinguished pupil was Aristotle, who arrived at the Academy at the age of 17 and stayed for 19 years, leaving only on Plato's death. However, Aristotle parted company from his master in many of his political views. Perhaps this had something to do with their different social backgrounds: Plato from the landed aristocracy, Aristotle from the professional middle class, his father having been a doctor.

A comparison of the two men's judgments on Sparta is instructive. We have already noticed that Aristotle shared Plato's distaste for Spartan militarism, and he naturally therefore objected to the practice of *krypteia*. He also shared with his teacher an admiration for the Spartan provision of public education rather than the usual private family arrangements. On the other hand, in the *Politics* (which we shall examine later) he presents a formidable list of criticisms of the Spartan constitution, customs and practices. In so doing he disagrees with Plato on the issue of the communistic features of Spartiate life. He observed that the allocation of land and the system of messes led in practice to the polarization of rich and poor citizens, not the equality that was the intention of the Lycurgan dispensation (see Aristotle, 1948, 1269b–1271b).

The contributions of Plato and Aristotle to the subject of citizenship are, furthermore, distinct in a more general, fundamental way than their responses to the Spartan experience. They had separate purposes in discoursing on the topic and therefore adopted different methodologies. Where Plato was primarily interested in drafting a blueprint for an ideal state, Aristotle was primarily interested in analysing actual constitutions and demonstrating the principles which underlay them. Aristotle's work on citizenship has, indeed, been far more influential than Plato's. It is time, therefore, for us to look at his contributions in their own right.

Aristotle spent about half his life in Athens, founding his own school, the Lyceum, in that city. Nevertheless, he was not an Athenian citizen. He was born, in 384 BC, on the border of Macedonia. He spent his childhood in the Macedonian capital and a little of his adult life there as tutor to the future Alexander the Great. Then, at the end of his life, because of anti-Macedonian feelings in Athens, he fled, and died in virtual exile in 322. Aristotle was an extraordinary polymath, though only two of his great range of works, which were probably in origin lectures, interest us here. Notwithstanding this limit in quantity, together the two books contain the finest analysis of the nature of citizenship in the whole classical tradition. The smaller contributions on the subject are a few scattered references in the *Nicomachean Ethics* (named after his father Nicomachus to distinguish it from two other works on ethics); the major fruits of Aristotle's analysis of citizenship are in his magisterial work on political matters, the *Politics*.

In summarizing this material, we shall take the following route through the texts. First we shall observe Aristotle tussling with the problem of defining citizenship. Then we shall notice his insistence that citizenship can operate effectively only in a compact community. From there we shall proceed to an examination of his notion of civic virtue. This relates to the use of education to produce the good citizen. And we shall conclude with some general commentary on the importance of his interpretation of our subject.

Aristotle famously declared that 'The nature of citizenship, like that of the state, is a question which is often disputed: there is no general agreement on a single definition' (Aristotle, 1948, 1275a). He then explains all the peripheral categories that would complicate the search for a universally acceptable working definition. These include: those resident aliens who have right of access to a state's courts; disenfranchised citizens; the young, who are 'undeveloped' citizens; and the old, who are 'superannuated'. (It may be noted in passing that, two-and-a-third millennia later, we are still no closer than Aristotle to managing the status of peripheral categories, notably resident aliens, in our attempts at shaping a modern definition of citizenship. We shall come to this current problem in due course. Politics is not exactly a progressive science!)

Nevertheless, Aristotle proffers three sets of guidelines. One concerns the naturalness of civic life. Another is his devising of a lowest common denominator of citizenship that is true for all states. And the third takes us into his consideration of civic virtue.

The most widely-known quotation from Aristotle is usually translated as 'man is a political animal'. The full statement, together with a more accurate rendering of Aristotle's meaning, is 'man is an animal impelled by his nature to live in a polis' (Aristotle, 1948, 1278b). Elsewhere he gives his message an added punch by means of a graphic assertion: 'The man who is isolated – who is unable to share in the benefits of political association, or has no need to share because he is already self-sufficient – is no part of the polis, and must therefore be either a beast or a god' (Aristotle, 1948, 1253a). The words 'nature' and '*polis*' are crucial. By 'nature' (the Greek word is '*physis*'), Aristotle means that, as the individual develops, so there grows the potential that is in him to participate in the affairs of the *polis*. But this natural participation can only really find effective expression in the compact and intimate context of the *polis*, a city-state of really quite small size consisting of an urban core and surrounding agricultural land. This was the normal form of the ancient Greek state.

However, what Aristotle was particularly interested in was the actual modes of participation that were common to all city-states – what makes a citizen a citizen. Two quotations get to the nub of the matter.

> Citizens, in the common sense of that term, are all who share in the civic life of ruling and being ruled in turn. In the particular sense of the term, they vary from constitution to constitution; and under an ideal constitution they must be those who are able and willing to rule with a view to attaining a way of life according to goodness.   (Aristotle, 1948, 1283b)

> [H]e who enjoys the right of sharing in deliberative and judicial office. . . attains thereby the status of a citizen of his state.   (Aristotle, 1948, 1275b)

There are several elements here, and an explanatory note or two on each will be helpful. 'Ruling and being ruled in turn' indicates a form of citizenship in which individuals are directly involved, in rotation: it is not just turning out to vote every few years if you feel so inclined. Who exactly are the totality ('all') of the citizenry and what form their 'ruling' takes inevitably depend on the form of constitution: a thorough-going democracy will involve more people wielding greater powers than a more restrictive form of state. Nevertheless, a good constitution operated by good citizens will ensure that the citizenly function will be discharged in the interest of all, not merely a segment of society.

But, what does 'ruling' entail? Aristotle is careful to embrace in his definition two forms of participation, the political and the judicial. In other words, the citizen should help to frame policy and laws by discussion and to operate the laws by making judgments. Common ways of fulfilling these duties would be attendance at an assembly and serving in civic offices, and membership of a jury respectively. The way in which these institutions worked will be explained through the example of Athens in the next section of this chapter.

Direct participation in civic affairs, the underlying principle of Aristotle's definitions, presupposes a small state. He is absolutely insistent on this point. It is not enough for him that there should be a limited number of citizens so that 'ruling in turn' is a practical possibility; the state must be of a geographically modest size too. Citizens must know each other, live together in a tightly-knit community. Only then can they know what is best for all and reach just judgments: 'Both in order to give decisions in matters of disputed rights, and to distribute the offices of government according to the merits of the candidates, the citizens of a state must know one another's characters' (Aristotle, 1948, 1326b).

The optimum size for a *polis*, he admits, is difficult to compute. However, in the *Ethics* he declares: 'Ten people would not make a city and a hundred thousand would exceed its natural proportions' (Aristotle, 1955, IX. 10). The context of this statement is Aristotle's discussion of friendship; for he believed that a special kind of civic friendship supplies the vital bonding which ensures that citizens work together in a spirit of mutual goodwill. The word he uses for this form of friendship is '*homonoia*' (concord). He explains:

> [Concord] is something more than agreement in opinion, for that might be found in people who do not know one another. . . we say that there is concord in a state when the citizens agree about their interests, adopt a policy unanimously and proceed to carry it out. . . . Now this conception of concord is realized among good men, for such are in harmony both with themselves and with one another. . . . But bad men. . . want more than their share. . . [and] shirk. . . public service. . . . The result is discord.   (Aristotle,1955, IX. 6)

So, Aristotle recognises that there are good citizens and bad citizens. Citizenship obviously works best when the citizens are good. And this brings us to Aristotle's views on *arete*, civic virtue, a concept, as we have already seen, that underpinned Spartan citizenship, though interpreted there in a particular way. What is Aristotle's interpretation? Just as the existence of multifarious constitutions presented him with the difficulty of drafting a definition of citizenship applicable to all, so the same situation raised a similar problem when it came to defining virtue. The good citizen must fit his behaviour to the requirements of the state; accordingly, for instance, where in one state vociferous involvement in an assembly would be good participation, in another it would be bad interference.

Having taken this into consideration, Aristotle expounds the four-fold content of virtue, as generally accepted by the Greeks. These four components are: temperance, that is, self-control, the avoidance of extremes; justice; courage, including patriotism; and wisdom, or prudence, including the capacity for judgment. A man possessed of these qualities will be a good citizen, will be capable of ruling well and of accepting the condition of being ruled. None the less, it may well seem a tall order to expect citizens to be such paragons. Certain it is that these virtues cannot be expected to develop in a citizen by natural moral growth; they must be cultivated by carefully devised education.

Aristotle and civic education

In our observations on Aristotle's attitude to Sparta, we noted his support for their public system of education. This was, for him, a cardinal principle. He declared that: 'the system of education in a state must. . . be one and the same for all, and the provision of the system must be a matter of public action.' The reason for this is directly related to his view of citizenship: 'We must not regard a citizen as belonging just to himself: we must rather regard every citizen as belonging to the state' (Aristotle, 1948, 1337aII). However, once again, Aristotle faced a dual task.

In the first place, he recognized the need for a flexible recommendation for citizenship education because of the great variety of political and social systems, which would require different educational preparations for their citizens. Young people in a democracy should be educated to be citizens supportive of a democracy, in an oligarchy (rule by a few), supportive of an oligarchy.

Secondly, he sought at the same time to offer general guiding principles. He lists the objectives:

> It is true that the citizens of our state must be able to lead a life of action and war; but they must be even more able to lead a life of leisure and peace. It is true, again, that they must be able to do good acts. These are the general aims which ought to be followed in the education of childhood and of the stages of adolescence which still require education.   (Aristotle, 1948, 1333a–b)

These objectives were not to be met by teaching 'academic' politics – unsuitable for young people lacking experience of the adult political world. No: Aristotle's advice was for a curriculum that would shape good moral character. Aesthetic and especially musical education should be used as the most efficacious subjects, for 'music possesses the power of producing an effect on the character of the soul' (Aristotle, 1948, 1340b).

Aristotle provided a coherent model of best practice adaptable to the variegated nature of Greek civic systems. Appropriate education will lead to a desire to act as a good, dutiful citizen, a life that can be effectively led only when the body of citizens form a real community.

His concept of citizenship was transmitted via adherents of the Stoic philosophy into Roman thinking on the subject, notably by Cicero. And although these ideas were submerged following the collapse of the Roman Empire, Aristotle's great corpus of works was rediscovered and revered in the Middle Ages with the result that his ideas on citizenship shaped the writings of a number of political philosophers, including Thomas Aquinas and Marsilius of Padua. Nor is his interpretation irrelevant to the very different forms of state in which we live today. Many political commentators and theorists have been searching for ways whereby the ideals of civic virtue, duties and community might be given greater salience in the complex pattern of contemporary citizenship. All that in due course; but for the moment we must stay in ancient Greece in order to focus on the first great exemplar of the democratic style of democracy, and Aristotle's adopted home, Athens.

Athens

The reformers

Aristotle thought deeply about the best kind of constitution. He very much favoured a mixed form: a measure of oligarchy (rule by the wealthy few), a little aristocracy (rule by the experienced best), topped up with some democracy (rule by the mass of the people). And he credited Solon with furnishing Athens with just such a mixed constitution. Solon was the great law-giver of Athens, the equivalent of Sparta's Lycurgus; but, in Solon's case there is plenty of evidence for his actual existence and for his authorship of the reforms associated with his name. He was born c.640 BC and introduced his reforms when he was in his late forties. These changes affected much of Athenian life, though, of course, only those provisions concerning citizenship are germane to our purposes.

One of the most useful sources for the history and working of Athenian citizenship is a study, *The Athenian Constitution*, which was probably written by one of Aristotle's students under his supervision. This text tells us that Solon gave citizens easier access to the law than hitherto and classified them in the following manner:

> He divided the citizens into four classes by an assessment of wealth, as they had been divided before: the five-hundred bushel class, the cavalry, the rankers and the labourers. He distributed among the five-hundred-bushel class and the cavalry and the rankers the major offices. . . , assigning offices to the members of each class according to the level of their assessment. To those registered in the labourers' class he gave only membership of the assembly and jury-courts.   (Aristotle, 1984, 7.3)

The three top classes by wealth – reckoned in dry and liquid measurements of produce – were relatively privileged. Nevertheless, membership of the Assembly and jury-courts – the sole privileges of the lowest class – were still very real citizenship rights. The description of these classes is rounded off with a nice little touch: because members of the lowest group were ineligible for public office, 'even today, when a candidate for allotment to any office is asked which class he belongs to, no one will reply that he belongs to the labourers' class' (Aristotle, 1984, 7.3). Despite the resultant social mobility of Solon's reforms, which allowed the poor, by acquisition of wealth, to rise in the hierarchy of citizen classes, and despite the collapse of these regulations through later democratic changes, the stigma of Solon's divisions of the citizenry persisted.

Further reforms were forthcoming at the end of the sixth century, devised by the *archon* (chief civilian official), Cleisthenes. His measures are usually taken as the inauguration of the Athenian democratic age, i.e. 508–322.

We must pause a while on this word 'democratic', for it has become a deceptively easy word in everyday discourse. 'Democracy' derives from two Greek words, *demos* (people) and *kratos* (rule); and we, by and large, believe that good government is based on the will of the people, that ultimate political power should lie with the people as a whole. Forms of government by a single person, a class, a party or a clique that cannot be challenged or overturned by the totality or majority of the state's citizens are less desirable. However, the matter is not quite as simple as that, and the Greeks, notably Aristotle, understood this. A democratic mode of government can be debased, the people swayed by demagogues into demanding foolish policies or using the force of their numbers to bring about political or social instability. Also, democracy is not an absolute, but an ingredient: a state can be more or less democratic, depending on its constitutional structure and the way that structure is articulated. Thus, although Cleisthenes introduced significant democratic features, Athens became more thoroughly democratic in the mid-fifth century when others, notably Pericles, advanced the process of democratization.

To return to Cleisthenes: his reforms were based on a rather complicated clustering of citizens into various groupings, cutting across the ancient clan allegiances and Solon's four classes. The process involved both the territory and the population.

The state (*polis*) of Athens consisted of the whole of Attica (about half the size of Luxembourg), not just the city. Cleisthenes divided this area into three 'regions': City, Inland and Coastal. Each of these regions was sub-divided into ten 'thirds', thirty in all.

The citizen body, formerly divided into four 'tribes', were now reorganized into ten tribes, in the words of *The Athenian Constitution*, 'to mix them up so that more men should have a share in the running of the state' (Aristotle, 1984, 21.1). Thus, we have thirty thirds and ten tribes. Cleisthenes allocated three thirds, one in each of the three regions, to each of the tribes.

Figure 1.2. Organization of Athenian citizens

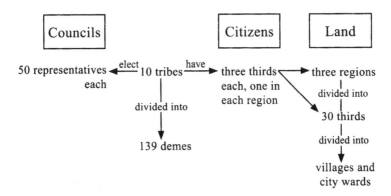

At the base of this structure, the whole citizen population was divided into 139 'demes'. Population figures are difficult to come by, but let us say that very roughly each deme was composed of about 200 citizens. It was this local unit, under the guidance of an official, the 'demarch', that provided the administrative groundwork of, and the citizens' 'on-the-job' training in, Athenian democracy.

Two other constitutional changes effected by Cleisthenes should be noted. One was the matching of the membership of the Council to the new structure of tribes. (The Council was the body that prepared business for the Assembly of all citizens.) The number of members was increased to 500, so that each tribe provided 50. The second constitutional innovation was the introduction of the power of ostracism, which was used in the fifth century. Each year the Assembly could censure one man, for example, a politician of whose policy they disapproved. Ostracism was a relatively mild form of punishment – it did not involve loss of citizenship: just ten years' exile!

In the middle of the fifth century some other changes were introduced to strengthen the powers of the Assembly. Also of importance was the introduction by Pericles of payments for attendance at the jury-courts, so that the poor would be able to exercise this citizenly right. However, he reduced the number of citizens by a law requiring that the status be restricted to legitimate sons of Athenian mothers as well as fathers. There was not a little irony in this law. Cleisthenes, the great reformer and uncle of Pericles' wife, would not have been an Athenian citizen if this regulation had existed in his time. Even more ironic, Pericles' only legitimate sons died in the horrendous plague of Athens (just before Pericles himself succumbed). He therefore had to suffer the humiliation of appealing to the Assembly to waive his own law in order to accord citizenship to his bastard sons, born to Pericles' mistress from the city of Miletus on the coast of Asia Minor!

The principles of Athenian democracy

The proof of these cumulative reforms is to be found in how the Athenians practised their citizenship. However, before analysing the constitution-in-practice, it will be helpful to explain three basic principles which underlay Athenian democracy. These were: the ideal of equality, the enjoyment of liberty, and the belief in participation.

Soon after the outbreak of what was to be the agonizingly long Peloponnesian War (431–404) between Athens and Sparta, Pericles, the great democratic politician, delivered a famous Funeral Oration over the bodies of fallen Athenian troops. In this speech he compared Sparta and Athens – very much, naturally, to the advantage of the latter – portraying the splendid attributes of its democratic system. He had this to say about the principle of equality:

> When it is a question of settling private disputes, everyone is equal before the law; when it is a question of putting one person before another in positions of public responsibility, what counts is not membership of a particular class, but the actual ability which the man possesses. No one, so long as he has it in him to be of service to the state, is kept in political obscurity because of poverty.   (Thucydides, 1954, p. 117)

We shall observe the principle of equality in practice below: participation in the Assembly, and the selection mechanism of lot rather than election.

Closely connected in the Greek mind to equality was freedom – freedom of thought, speech and action. The relationship of this principle to Athenian citizenship is two-fold, and can be dated to the early fifth century. The first aspect was awareness of the value of freedom. The wars between Greece and Persia were a frightening experience for the Greeks and made them, particularly the Athenians, highly conscious of the differences between the contending sides. The Persians were perceived as 'barbarians', living under a political tyranny; the Athenians, in contrast, lived cultivated lives in a constitutional system in which freedom was cherished. As Pericles later declared of Athenians: 'each single one of our citizens, in all the manifold aspects of life, is able to show himself the rightful lord and owner of his own person' (Thucydides, 1954, p. 119). That freedom had to be preserved at all costs.

But – and this is the second aspect – the Athenians, following the reforms of Cleisthenes, adopted a very particular kind of freedom, so particular that they invented a separate word for it, *parrhesia*. This was freedom of speech, and was, of course, vital if the Assembly was to operate in a truly democratic way. Without freedom to speak one's mind and to participate with impunity in the execution of popularly determined policies there can be no democratic citizenship.

However, an atmosphere of freedom, while necessary, is not sufficient for an effective democratic citizenship. The citizens themselves must in addition have the will-power to exercise that freedom in a positive way. They must participate in discussing with their fellow-citizens the issues of the day in the market-square-cum-gathering place (*agora*); and they must be keen to discharge their duties through the institutions of government and justice. Moreover, it is through this participation that we see the connection between freedom and equality: Athenian citizens engaged in these activities as equals, despite the continuation of Solon's class divisions. Pericles expressed his pride in this trait of his fellow-citizens:

> Here each individual is interested not only in his own affairs but in the affairs of the state as well: even those who are mostly occupied with their own business are extremely well-informed on general politics – this is a peculiarity of ours: we do not say that a man who takes no interest in politics is a man who minds his own business; we say he has no business at all. We Athenians, in our own persons, take our decisions on policy or submit them to proper discussions: for we do not think that there is an incompatibility between words and deeds. (Thucydides, 1954, p. 118)

Athenian democracy in practice

By no means all the inhabitants of Attica were citizens. Athenian democracy was democratic only in the sense of the equality, freedom and participation of those who were citizens in the full sense of the word. How, then, was the population divided?

During the fifth and fourth centuries BC the number of citizens is reckoned to have been about 30,000 (expanding temporarily in the middle of that period to 50,000 or so). This figure must be multiplied by about four to account for children and wives to give the total of those in the citizenly category – only men were citizens proper. In addition to the citizens were many thousands of both metics and slaves. Metics were immigrants, short-stay and permanent, who were legally free and enjoyed some limited rights and were subject to obligations of military service and taxation. The slaves were, of course, by definition, unfree.

There is a further complication in surveying the Athenian population, for, although the principle of equality before the law and of political opportunity obtained for citizens, that body of men must not be understood as being entirely homogeneous. Solon's classes persisted, involving a distinction in the form of military service below the cavalry class. (We should remember, after all, that citizenship, even in democratic Athens, entailed military as well as civilian duties.) The third class were hoplites (heavy infantry), while the fourth, lowest class, who could not afford to buy the hoplite's equipment, served as auxiliaries or in the navy. There was also division by age. From 18 to 20 youths of citizen families undertook military training and duties. And from 20 to 30 young men had partial citizen rights, able to attend the Assembly but not to hold office.

The induction of a young man into the status and role of citizen began when he was eighteen. The Athenian year started in mid-summer; and on the first day of the new year after the youth's eighteenth birthday his application for citizenship was considered by the members of his deme. The deme members checked that he was eligible by birth and age; then, if his credentials were accepted as valid, the deme members voted and swore to that validity on oath. If a youth was proved to have made a false application and his appeal was rejected, he was sold as a slave.

The newly-enrolled cadets (*epheboi*) swore an oath: 'I will leave my country not less, but greater and better, than I found it. I will obey the magistrates and observe the existing laws, and those the people may hereafter make. If anyone tries to overthrow or disobey the ordinances, I will resist him in their defence' (see Boyd, 1932, pp. 21–2). Then, from *c*.335, a period of compulsory 'national service' was introduced, at first for two years, later reduced to one. The two-year programme was structured along the following lines. The cadets were placed in the charge of three officers chosen by the tribes and a commander chosen from the whole citizen body, as well as instructors in the various martial skills. Some of the cadets undertook guard duties. At the end of his first year each cadet was presented with a spear and a shield and spent his second year on frontier patrol and guard duties.

At the age of thirty the Athenian citizen became eligible for jury-service. The procedure for trials was extraordinarily complicated and changed over the centuries. What follows is a very simplified summary of the jury system in the fourth century. Each year about 6,000 citizens, chosen by lot, were registered as a panel of jurors. Arrangements were based on the ten tribes – for example, the courts had ten entrances. Each juror had his own wooden ticket identifying him by name and deme. The number of jurors enpanelled for a particular trial was huge by present-day standards: 201 or 401 for private cases; for public trials 501 was normal; twice or even three times that number for big, important cases.

Citizens who presented themselves at the courts for jury-service were selected, according to the number required, by lot, thus eliminating any possibility of 'packing' juries. Court officials were also selected by lot. At the end of the proceedings the jurors voted by ballot to indicate whether they supported the plaintiff's case or the defendant's. Having cast his ballot, the juror's ticket was returned to him (surrendered at the start of the selection) as proof that he had completed his duty. On showing this he received his stipend for the day, the payment introduced, as we have seen, by Pericles. The rate was three obols. Since, by the late fourth century an unskilled labourer could earn three times that amount for a day's work, only the very poor or elderly found the remuneration attractive.

In 422 BC the young playwright Aristophanes staged his knock-about farce, *The Wasps*, satirically caricaturing this outcome. The main character, the old man Procleon, is a jury-junkie. One of the household slaves tells another: 'Oh, he did have it badly: as soon as supper was over he'd shout for his shoes, and off he'd go to the court, and sleep through the small hours at the head of the queue, clinging to the doorpost like a limpet' (Aristophanes, 1964, p .43). Part of the attraction is the payment, but part is the sense of power. Procleon gloats:

Can you think of any living creature that is happier, more fortunate, more pampered, or more feared than a juror? No sooner have I crawled out of bed in the morning than I find great hulking fellows waiting for me at the bar of the court. . . , and they all bow down low, and plead with me in pitiful tones. . . . Then, after they've. . . tried to soften me up, I go behind the bar and take my seat, and forget all about any promises I may have made.   (Aristophanes, 1964, pp. 57–8)

The citizenry of Athens not only worked the jury-courts judicial system; they also operated the political system of the Council, the Principal Assembly (the standing committee of the Council) and the Assembly.

All citizens had the right to attend meetings of the Assembly: this was the fundamental feature of Athenian democracy – direct involvement, not the election of representatives. The usual attendance was about 6,000, though, naturally, matters of really signal importance drew larger numbers. The meetings were mostly held, obviously, in view of the numbers, in the open, on the Pnyx, a hill to the west of the Acropolis. In order to encourage attendance, in the fourth century, payment was made at the rate of one drachma, that is, twice the stipend for jury-service.

The Assembly has been considered the hub and epitome of Athenian democratic citizenship. By personal attendance, every citizen had the right and opportunity – indeed, the responsibility – to shape the life of the *polis*, because the agendas spanned the whole range of business, from momentous matters of high policy to the minutiae of public administration. The Assembly elected generals, initiated legislation and held all the officials to account at the end of their year's office. Moreover, because many thousands held the status of citizen, every class and social and economic interest had a voice; indeed, the rural and urban manual workers being the most numerous had, at least potentially, the greatest weight when it came to the vote. Socrates, in fact, ridiculed the Assembly as a collection of 'laundry men, shoemakers, carpenters, smiths, peasants, merchants, and shopkeepers' (see Lloyd-Jones, 1965, p. 72). On the other hand, those most knowledgeable about public affairs and most articulate could dominate the proceedings. Meetings normally lasted about two hours, at the end of which, decisions were reached by a show of hands, assessed, not counted.

Day-to-day administration was in the hands of 1,200 magistrates (civil officials), the great majority of whom were chosen by lot from those citizens who stood for office. Impersonal lottery was thought preferable to election because it eliminated the possibility of bribery, which is corrosive of democratic processes. This group provided the membership of the Council of Five Hundred – 50 from each tribe – which oversaw the detailed running of the *polis*.

Athens, then, in its democratic age, was a state governed and administered not by professional politicians and civil servants but by its amateur citizens: government by lottery, if one wishes to be dubiously critical – as aristocrats and philosophers such as Plato certainly were. Even so, the system was not as haphazard as its critics believed. The Assembly would usually have had a shrewd collective understanding of the wisest course of action to pursue. Even Aristotle, no lover of democracy, admitted that 'There is this to be said for the Many. Each of them by himself may not be of good quality; but when they all come together it is possible that they may surpass – collectively and as a body. . . – the quality of the few best. . . each can bring his share of goodness and moral prudence' (Aristotle, 1948, 1281a–b). What is more, during a lifetime, Athenian citizens who took an interest in public affairs would accumulate considerable experience – as jurymen, councillors and magistrates. After all, there were literally thousands of opportunities for participation.

However, involvement in the institutions of the central government, administration and judiciary, even in the small scale of a city-state, is not the be-all and end-all of citizenship. The practice of citizenship at the grass-roots – at the basic unit of village, parish or ward in today's terms – is vital, both for its own sake and for an understanding of and a preparation for participation at the 'higher' levels. In Athens that crucial function was performed by the demes. Each of the village demes behaved as a kind of *polis* in microcosm. They passed their own decrees, which we might think of as by-laws, and constructed their own *agorae*, public gathering-places for the discussion of the affairs of the deme. No doubt many an Athenian citizen would have been reluctant to travel to the city to perform his duties there. Yet, by conscientious engagement in the affairs of his deme he would have kept alive and healthy the ideals, principles and activities of a style of citizenship which we can still admire two-and-a-half millennia later.

That style was dependent in both theory and practice on the intimacy of a compact community. Rome, too, like the Greek *poleis*, started as a city-state. But were the Romans able to adapt their form of citizenship to the vastly wider dimensions of an Empire?

CHAPTER TWO

Rome

Republic and Empire

Origins and status of Roman citizenship

Roman citizenship was in many of its features strikingly different from the Greek. The Roman citizenly status became far more flexible as it evolved than its Greek equivalent. The Romans instituted citizenship of various grades; afforded opportunities to slaves to acquire the dignity of citizen; and spread the title with exceeding generosity to individuals, to whole communities even, beyond the city, in due course, to the very confines of its 'world empire'.

The origins of the Roman citizenship are even mistier than the Greek: no great law-giver like Solon, not even a semi-mythical figure like Lycurgus. We know that there was citizenship in some sense in the very early years of the Republic (the monarchy was abolished c.507 BC), attained through the struggle of the ordinary folk of Rome (the plebs or plebeians) to obtain rights against the privileged (the patricians).

A key date is 494. In that year the plebeians as a body marched out of Rome and up the Aventine Hill to the south of the city. They swore an oath of mutual support and affirmed their determination to extract from the patricians the appointment of officials to safeguard plebeian interests. Fearing social instability and the disintegration of the army, the patricians succumbed to the pressure. Thus were appointed the first Tribunes of the People – a remarkable concession to protect the plebs from abuses and injustice. These Tribunes were elected by a new popular Assembly, though its powers were weak and it was short-lived. The fight to secure an effective voice in an Assembly is a long and complex story, which we shall outline shortly.

The enjoyment and protection of rights and the creation of institutions for the voicing of opinions and demands are signs of embryonic citizenship. But some means must exist to identify those who are eligible for the status: a Roman citizen had to be distinguished from a man who was of more lowly status, or was unfree, or was illegitimate, or who was a foreigner.

Originally, a simple ceremony sufficed: the citizen-father would pick up his new-born child as an act of recognition. Later, this family acknowledgment was formalized by the tribal lists of all adult citizens compiled and scrutinized by the Censors every five years. From 44 BC all local magistrates were required to compile full and detailed lists of citizens for the purpose of taxation and military service. Then, in 4 BC, by a law of Augustus, the registration of births was made compulsory. All children of citizens had to be registered in the presence of an official within 30 days of birth. The fact of registration was recorded on a two-panelled wooden 'certificate' of citizenship. Different recording methods were used on the enfranchisement of military and civilian adults.

What, then, did it entail being a citizen of Rome? At its heart the status meant that the individual lived under the guidance and protection of Roman law. This affected both his private and his public life, irrespective of whether he had any interest in political participation or not.

The Roman citizenship was shaped by a pattern of duties and rights. The duties were basically military service and the payment of certain taxes. These latter were mainly levies on property and inheritance tax; though, it must be said that Roman taxation policy throughout its history and across the extent of its Empire was a topic of bewildering complexity.

However, behind the specific obligations of citizenship lay the ideal of civic virtue (*virtus*) analogous to the Greek concept of *aretē*. Life, of course, did not always come up to the expectations of the ideal. Nevertheless, stories from 'olden times' kept the image alive. One of the most famous concerned a man named Cincinnatus. After a distinguished public life, he retired to tend his small three-acre farm. But a crisis arose in 458 BC in the conflict between Rome and the Aequi, a people living some miles to the east of Rome, and the Roman government judged that Cincinnatus was the best man to save the city from disaster. He was given supreme power for six months, defeated the Aequi in fifteen days, then returned to his plough and his simple life, refusing any reward. He had discharged his citizenly duty – that was sufficient.

Even so, duties were balanced by rights. And here the distinction between the private and the public spheres of life are clear. Under the private heading we may list the right to marry into another citizen family and the right to trade with another Roman citizen, rights denied to non-citizens. Moreover, the taxes levied on citizens were lighter than those exacted from non-citizens. In addition, as citizenship spread throughout the provinces beyond Italy, especially in Imperial times, a citizen enjoyed protection against the authority of a provincial Governor. For example, if a citizen was accused of any offence, he could claim the privilege of trial in Rome.

Public or political rights of citizenship were of three kinds: to vote for members of the Assemblies and for candidates to political office (the magistrates, e.g. Consuls, Praetors); to sit in the Assemblies; and to become a magistrate – though class divisions in practice inhibited any real equality of opportunity.

Turning our attention to the Assemblies, it is necessary to explain that Roman citizens never experienced the kind of political power wielded by the Athenian citizens in their Assembly in that state's democratic era. Rome was never a democracy. In Republican times power rested in the hands of the Senate and Consuls; in Imperial times, of the Emperor.

Nevertheless, some popular influence was exerted by elected Assemblies. One was the *comitia curiae*, based upon family clan groupings. This was effectively superseded by the *comitia centuriata*, elected by men of military age in their legionary units, called centuries. This Assembly, dominated, because of voting procedures, by the wealthy classes, had a range of powers, including the election of magistrates. However, yet a third Assembly came into being, the *comitia tributa*, based upon 'tribal' divisions. These were voting wards and settled down to 35 in number in 241 BC. By that time this Assembly had secured powers to make laws, though it was scarcely the authentic voice of Roman citizens.

The principle of Assembly meetings was that of a city-state citizenry, as in Athens, for example. No adaptations were made to keep up with changing circumstances. Yet by the mid-third century BC there were hundreds of thousands of Roman citizens in territory stretching from Rome to the Adriatic Sea. Not many would have the time, interest or money to make the journey to the city when the Assembly was convened, even though, to encourage attendance, meetings were forbidden on market days. Furthermore, as Rome extended her sway over the whole of the Mediterranean basin it was utterly impossible to sustain the right of attendance. And, in any case, the centralization of power in the person of the Emperor in the Imperial age completely emasculated the Assembly. Only two pieces of legislation emanating from the Assembly are recorded after the reign of Tiberius (d. AD 37).

None the less, despite this lack of any really great influence even at the height of the popular Assembly's constitutional authority, in Republican times the title of Roman citizen was much sought-after; and the declaration *'Civis Romanus sum'* (I am a Roman citizen) was an expression of pride. Acquisition of citizenship afforded several benefits, as we have already seen; conversely, the acquisition of extra citizens was of benefit to the Roman state because the status secured their loyalty and their potential recruitment as legionaries.

And so it came about that the Roman citizenship spread beyond the confines of the city. By *c*.600 BC the little settlements on the River Tiber had coagulated into the city-state of Rome. A century later Rome was starting to conquer some of her neighbours. She was consequently faced with the problem of how to manage an expanding state – a problem that was to continue into the Imperial age.

Expansion of citizenship in Italy

Within half a century, during the course of their conquest of Latium (the territory to the south-east of Rome), the Romans made two cardinal decisions, which rendered possible the future massive extension of Roman citizenship.

The first of these decisive innovations was implemented in 381 BC. In that year the Latin city of Tusculum, independent but by then surrounded by Roman territory, was adopting a hostile stance against Rome. The question was: Should Rome react in a conciliatory or aggressive manner? The peaceful road was chosen. The citizens of Tusculum were offered full Roman citizenship while maintaining their own municipal form of government. It was an unprecedented arrangement and was to be often repeated thereafter. In fact, as Rome steadily spread its control over Latium, then the rest of Italy, it eschewed vindictive peace settlements with those it conquered.

In 338 Rome invented the second device – a kind of second class or semi-citizenship, a less generous provision than that which had been afforded to Tusculum. It came about in this way. From 340 to 338 Rome fought a fearsome war with her neighbours of Latium and Campania, the Latin War. At its conclusion the participant Latin towns were treated differently, but the citizens of seven of them were given a new status. The Latin term is '*civitas sine suffragio*', citizenship without the vote (or the right to hold office as a Roman magistrate).

It was a clever scheme, providing the institution of Roman citizenship with maximum flexibility. The kernel of the arrangement was the understanding that citizenship has two faces, the public and the private. The former aspect, the right to vote in elections, was withheld; the latter, for example, the right to trade on equal terms with a Roman or to marry a Roman, was given. And, of course, it was always possible – as, indeed, in due course happened – for the *civitas sine suffragio* of an individual or a whole community to be upgraded to full citizenship.

There were other, less important, devices also that were used to expand the numbers holding some form of Roman citizenship so that by the mid-third century BC the whole of central Italy was embraced in these arrangements. However, during the second century the pace of citizenship conferment was slowed down, leading by *c*.100 to resentment among towns of Italy who held the status of Allies of Rome and who lived in expectation of receiving the citizenship. Together with other causes of friction, this issue provoked a ferocious war which lasted from 91 to 87 and cost an estimated 300,000 lives. This conflict is called the 'Social War', confusingly; the reason for the term is that the Latin word for allies is '*socii*'.

Just as the Latin War brought changes, so the Social War forced the Romans to take stock of their citizenship policy. In order to reward and keep the loyalty of those communities who refrained from joining the belligerent Allies, and, crucially, to induce some of the Allies to lay down their arms, Rome passed the *lex Julia* in 90 BC. This law conferred citizenship, admittedly in limited form only, on probably hundreds of thousands throughout Italy. Even the rebels benefited after the war. Roman citizenship was now something like a 'national' status, by no means confined geographically to the city of Rome itself.

By the end of the Republican era opportunities had been extended throughout the whole of the peninsula for the bestowal of citizenship in one form or another. Julius Caesar introduced the status into the Gallic lands of northern Italy. His policy regarding citizenship was, indeed, to extend it quite generously both within Italy and beyond. He enfranchised medical practitioners in Rome, for example. However, the more ambitious idea of substantial geographical extension of the status was postponed until the Imperial era.

Expansion of citizenship beyond Italy

Before chronicling the expansion of citizenship beyond the Italian peninsula, we must pause to investigate an interesting problem relating to the conquest of communities which already had their own highly developed civic lives, including the status of citizen. Could a man hold two citizenships? Could he be simultaneously a citizen of his native city and of Rome? The question was raised as early as 56 BC by that most distinguished Roman scholar-lawyer, Cicero. (It is also a matter that has exercised lawyers in the twentieth century as they have devised rulings on dual nationality.)

In that year Cicero argued in a legal case that the strain on a man's loyalty meant that citizenship of another city was incompatible with the status of Roman citizenship: a man had to choose. The case arose because Pompey conferred Roman citizenship on one Cornelius Balbo, a citizen of Gades (modern Cadiz). Habit, Cicero argued, may have come to condone dual citizenship; the law of Rome certainly did not:

> Now all other states would, without hesitation, bestow their citizenship upon our citizens, if we had the same system of law as themselves. . . . Thus we see that citizens of Athens, Rhodes, Sparta, and of other states far and wide, are enrolled as citizens of Greek states, and that the same persons are citizens of many states. And I myself have seen certain ignorant men, citizens of ours, misled by this, sitting at Athens amongst jurymen and members of the Areopagus [Council of senior citizens]. . . since they did not know that if they acquired citizenship there, they had forfeited it here.   (Cicero, 1958, pp. 29–30)

None the less, during the course of the century following this speech, this regulation was increasingly flouted. For example, in c.58 AD a man was arrested in Palestine. He declared himself to be 'a Jew of Tarsus, a city in Cilicia, a citizen of no mean city' (Acts 21.39). Tarsus was a Greek city in this province of Asia Minor. The man was being prepared for a whipping when he claimed the privilege of Roman citizenship, which he also held, and which forbade such treatment. And because of this status also he was sent to Rome for trial. In the event, after many vicissitudes, he was executed for his dangerous and unpopular religious beliefs, a fate from which his Roman citizenship did not protect him. This man was Jesus Christ's disciple St Paul.

After this diversion it behoves us now to return to pick up our chronological narrative at the Principate of Augustus. Three main phases in the process of increasing the number of citizens may be identified. First, the policy of Augustus (27 BC– AD 14). He rewarded troops who were not already citizens (in fact, many were) by the award of citizenship on their discharge. He also generally added to the citizen rolls. By including their families as well as the adult male citizens in the numbers of citizenly rank, we reach a figure of over one million enfranchised by Augustus, most in non-Italian provinces. As a very approximate estimate this was seven per cent of the total population of the Empire.

We may insert here a case of somewhat black irony, illustrating perhaps a too lax allocation of citizenship at this time. In AD 9 the Roman army suffered its most devastating and humiliating defeat. Three legions and accompanying cavalry were cut to pieces in the Teutoburg Forest. The victor was Arminius (Herman), chieftain of the German Cherusci people, and who became a great hero of the German nationalists of the nineteenth century. He was a Roman citizen!

The second phase in the history of the Imperial donation of citizenship embraces the reigns of Claudius (41–54) and Hadrian (117–138). Claudius not only bestowed citizenship on many non-Italians, he encouraged Gauls in particular to enter the Senate and take up political offices.

But it was the Emperor Caracalla (211–217) who promulgated the most famous of all laws relating to Roman citizenship, in the *Constitutio Antoniania* (the Antonine Constitution) of 212. Virtually all the various geographical exceptions and variations in grades of citizenship disappeared in this significant act of simplification, which in effect embraced all the free inhabitants of the Empire in the citizenly status. The edict had particular impact on the provinces, where, unlike Italy, citizenship had previously been largely confined to a small elite. Caracalla had, in fact, pushed through to their logical and tidy conclusion the policies of his predecessors of piecemeal extensions.

The Antonine Constitution was a great symbolic measure. Yet we must not exaggerate its real effects, for it was neither altruistic in intent nor revolutionary in outcome. Four points should be noted. The first is Caracalla's purpose. Only citizens were subject to inheritance tax, so, by substantially increasing the numbers of citizens he substantially enhanced the funds available for military expenditure – his overriding concern. Also, at the same time, he doubled the rate of that tax!

The second observation is that the constant extensions of the status of citizen, which Caracalla capped, debased the value of the once proudly owned title. Once anyone could be a citizen it was no longer a badge of distinction; and the degrading of the status drew some bitter comments. The philosopher Seneca had written with heavy sarcasm about the citizenship policy of Claudius. He pictured Clotho, the Fate who spins each individual's thread of life, standing by the Emperor's deathbed, but delaying the final moment, saying to the impatient messenger Mercury,

> I had thought to give him a few more minutes so that he might bestow the citizenship on the handful of men who have not already received it (for he has determined to see all Greeks, Gauls, Spaniards, and Britons clad in the toga), but that some foreign harvest may be left for

the future, you can have it your own way.   (quoted, Hadow, 1923, p. 12)

Thirdly, gradually during the first two centuries AD the distinction between a citizen and a free non-citizen was being eroded. Citizens' privileges were lost – even the right to vote – and non-citizens' rights were increased. Moreover, such was the need for maintaining the strength of the legions that it became necessary to recruit non-citizens into the army.

However, and fourthly, this decay of the distinctiveness of the citizenship must not be interpreted as a process of equalization. Far from it. By the time of Caracalla's edict, class divisions between the superior class (*honestiores*) and the lower orders (*humiliores*) had become hardened. The citizens of the lower category suffered not only inferior legal rights but also punishments which had in earlier centuries been meted out only to non-citizens. What price then the proud boast encapsulated in Cicero's tag, *Civis Romanus sum*?

'Caracalla' was in fact a nickname: his full Imperial name was Marcus Aurelius Antoninus (hence the title of his edict). Fifty years before he became Emperor a man with exactly the same name, known to history as Marcus Aurelius, was made Emperor (161–180). Not only was he a conscientious ruler, he was a notable philosopher of the Stoic school too. In that capacity he had thoughtful comments to make on citizenship. Indeed, Stoicism requires a section of its own.

Stoics

Theory and practice

In 310 BC Zeno, who hailed from Citium, a city on the south coast of Cyprus, but who had settled in Athens, attracted students to his house in order to expound his new, all-embracing philosophy. He held these seminars in his covered painted porch. Hence the name of what became a long-lived school of philosophy – Stoicism; the Greek for 'painted porch' is '*stoa poikele*'. Interest in and the influence of Stoicism came in three waves, very roughly, 300 BC, 100 BC and AD 100.

From this philosophy, which embraced all spheres of knowledge and enquiry, we need to extract just two themes. One is the stern requirements of dedication to the state and of duty to undertake public service: civic virtue of the highest order. The other is the belief that one should be a world citizen by living in accordance with a universal moral code of good conduct. Stoicism therefore taught that the individual as a virtuous political being must be loyal, and feel a deep loyalty to both his state and the universal natural law. For he is a member of both the *polis*, the 'city', the legally, constitutionally existent state, and the *cosmopolis*, the 'world city', a metaphorical, notional universal moral community. But were these dual loyalties reconcilable? Would not Cicero's principle of incompatibility come into play to shatter the twin Stoic ideal? Would it not be even harder to juggle allegiance to Rome and the universe than to Rome and Gades?

We shall examine each of these three ideas, namely, duty to the state, commitment to universal moral law and the problem of their reconciliation. And we shall draw upon three Roman writers to exemplify each of these matters. These will be Cicero, Marcus Aurelius and Seneca, respectively. Now it happens that these three men not only wrote on Stoic political philosophy; they also lived their lives conscientiously according to Stoic precepts. A little biographical detail will demonstrate this, and for this purpose we shall take them in chronological order.

Although, unlike Seneca and Marcus Aurelius, Cicero cannot be categorized as a Stoic philosopher, he none the less interested himself in this school of thought and expressed many of its ideas in his works. He made particularly notable contributions to the ideas of natural law and civic duty. He was also an eminent lawyer and orator and played an active part in politics. Indeed, he died stoically pursuing what he believed to be Rome's best interests. He was born in 106 BC. When he was quite elderly – in 44 – Julius Caesar was assassinated. It looked decidedly possible that Mark Antony would take control of Rome and destroy the Republican constitution and political values. Cicero bitterly and very publicly opposed Mark Antony, who dispatched his 'hitmen' to kill him.

Just over a century later, in AD 65 Seneca committed suicide rather than be executed by the Emperor Nero, who believed the philosopher to have been implicated in a plot to overthrow him. Seneca was, in truth, appalled by the accumulating evidence of the Emperor's vicious and sacrilegious behaviour. Like Cicero, Seneca combined writing with public duty. He held magistrates' offices and, on Nero's accession, became the Emperor's political adviser, yet also managed an active literary output, making distinguished contributions to the spread of Stoicism.

Just over half a century after the death of Seneca the man who was to become the Emperor Marcus Aurelius was born. He was a precocious child, determined at the age of 12 to dedicate himself to the study of philosophy. However, he was born into a politically active family and, no doubt with some reluctance, was drawn into public life too. He worked hard, especially as Emperor, and died at the relatively early age of 59. But his fame rests less on the execution of his political and military duties than on the private jotting-down of his personal thoughts. Two centuries later they became known and are usually given the title of his *Meditations*. An amalgam of several philosophies, they exhibit a considerable strain of Stoicism.

Three citizenship issues

By drawing on the writings of these three famous exponents of Stoicism we can highlight three particularly important issues regarding citizenship that are raised by the philosophy.

First, the matter of civic duty. Zeno's *stoa* is preserved in the English language through the words 'stoically' and 'stoicism', indicating an uncomplaining commitment to fulfilling one's duties, responsibilities and obligations. The Stoic philosophy indeed laid stress on this age-old feature of citizenship in a manner reminiscent of the Spartan interpretation of *arete*. There is, as we have seen in Chapter One, always the problem whether all citizens can be relied upon to display such demanding personal qualities. Perhaps only an elite can achieve this excellence? More than a hint of this point of view is to be found in Stoicism, which taught that the right mode of life is attainable only through the acquisition of wisdom, which in turn was obtained by the exercise of man's rational faculty.

Cicero reflects this selective view of civic duty. Moreover, he had good reason for this focus. By his time the ancient republican virtues, personified by the story of Cincinnatus, were in sad and worrying decline. The civic standards of the upper classes, who had always set an example, were decaying.

Cicero adjured them to mend their ways. Pulling no punches, he declared that men who lead private lives are 'traitors to social life' (quoted, Riesenberg, 1992, p. 77). (A comment that may be compared with Pericles' on the same topic.) And his message to the higher ranks of Roman citizens specifically was uncompromising: he wrote in an essay entitled *On Duties*:

> a worthy and truly brave citizen, and one who deserves to hold the reins of the government. . . will give himself so to the service of the public, as to aim at no riches or power for himself; and will so take care of the whole community, as not to pass over any part of it. . . [and]

will rather part with life itself, than do anything that is contrary to the virtues I have maintained.   (quoted, Clarke, 1994, p. 49)

The ideal of civic duty has been a common theme through our narrative thus far. The concept of world citizenship, on the other hand, now makes its first appearance, so some explanation of its meaning is called for at this point.

The conception of world citizenship presupposes a certain, at least potential, homogeneity of mankind; that all human beings have the capacity to recognize the superficiality of cultural or ethnic differences. Such a notion cut clean across the Greek belief that the world was composed of the cultured people who spoke Greek and those who did not, who babbled – the barbarians. Even so, the two interpretations of humanity – homogeneity and bifurcation – did manage to co-exist in Greek thought. The Stoics stressed the homogeneity of all men capable of reasoning.

The Greek word which is often translated as 'citizen of the world' is 'kosmopolites', but it is more accurately rendered as 'citizen of the cosmos' or 'universe'. All life forms, including the gods, not just humans, were encapsulated in that term. It is necessary to note this because Stoics like Marcus Aurelius, who passionately believed themselves to be citizens of the world, would have found it inconceivable to propound the need for a world state, of which they would be citizens. (Other than the Roman Empire, which at times, exhibited universalist pretensions of a vainglorious, not Stoic, kind.) Exponents of the idea of 'world citizenship' used the word 'citizen' to express themselves because it was the obvious one to hand, not because they imagined it to be taken literally.

But if they did not wish to convey that world citizenship existed or ought to exist in any literal sense, should we be at all interested in the notion in our task of describing the history of citizenship? The answer is a cautious affirmative, and derives from the element of morality in the citizenship principle. The belief in world citizenship challenges the view that the state has the monopoly of what is right, challenges Aristotle's assertion that man can achieve social and moral excellence only by membership of a *polis*. Cosmopolitanism asserts that there is another, higher criterion. At the turn of the second millennium AD the validity of this thought came to be re-emphasized, as we shall eventually show. Citizens must be conscious of this complication in their role.

Marcus Aurelius grasped this truth. He logically 'proved' that a *cosmopolis*, a city of the universe, exists as one of the Stoic principles, and asserted the unremitting duty of the good man to obey its code of conduct by another of its principles. Here are two extracts from his *Meditations* which clearly reveal his thinking.

> If the intellectual capacity is common to all, common too is the reason, which makes us rational creatures. If so, that reason is common which tells us to do or not to do. If so, law is common. If so, we are citizens. If so, we are fellow-members of an organized community. If so, the Universe is as it were a state – for of what other single polity can the whole race of mankind be said to be fellow-members? – and from it, this common State, we get the intellectual, the rational, and the legal instinct, or whence do we get them?

> [W]herever a man live, he live as a citizen of the World-City. Let men look upon thee, cite thee, as a man in very deed that lives according to Nature. If they cannot bear thee, let them slay thee. For it were better so than to live their life.   (Marcus Aurelius Antoninus, 1961, IV. 4, X. 15)

Marcus believed that as a citizen he belonged to Rome, as a man, to the Universe. But was it, could it be, as simple as that? Were not the two personalities and loyalties bound to conflict? If so, then surely Stoic political thinking contained a fundamental internal contradiction.

Seneca was alert to this problem, and displayed this understanding in both his writing and his life. He argued that 'there are two commonwealths – the one, a vast and truly common state, which embraces alike gods and men. . . the other, the one to which we have been assigned by the accident of birth'. Men owe duties to both; however, 'Some yield service to both commonwealths at the same time – to the greater and to the lesser – some only to the lesser, some only to the greater' (Seneca, 1958, IV.i).

Yet, although individuals may choose a priority, there is no serious contradiction. The reason for this judgment is that service to the *cosmopolis* is of a contemplative, self-educative kind. 'This greater commonwealth,' he wrote, 'we are able to serve even in leisure – nay, I am inclined to think, even better in leisure – so that we may inquire what virtue is' (Seneca, 1958, IV.i). During the last three years of his life he attempted precisely this – withdrawal from involvement in the earthly state – as he became aware of Nero's malignant character. But, as we have seen, his past as a public figure caught up with him.

Seneca's attempt at a dichotomy between the two kinds of citizenships found a clear echo in Christian thinking in Jesus' advice, 'Render unto Caesar the things which are Caesar's; and unto God the things that are God's' (St Matthew, 22.21). But, then, do God's things touch upon citizenship? If any era could link them it was surely the Middle Ages.

CHAPTER THREE

Medieval and Early Modern Periods

Middle Ages

Christianity

In the Graeco–Roman world, for something like half a millennium, citizenship was a cardinal feature of the form of government, way of life even. In medieval Europe – with the notable exception of the Italian city-states – citizenship was of relatively peripheral importance.

But insofar as the role of citizen was performed and the concept was commented upon, three elements are in evidence in this period. First was the relationship of citizenship to the unquestioned and effectively unquestionable pre-eminence and pervasiveness of Christianity. Secondly, the classical idea was not for ever lost; indeed, it was powerfully revived with a deep interest in Aristotle. Thirdly, in the Middle Ages, citizenship in practice meant a privileged status in a city or a town, not a state. This section considers each of these three characteristics. However, Italy represents a special case, to which a separate section has been allotted and which carries us forward to the Renaissance.

By the fifth century AD the Roman Empire in the west had collapsed; 'barbarian' kingdoms of, for example, Anglo-Saxons, Vandals and Goths were being consolidated on its ruins. No Roman Empire, no Roman citizenship; for in the east, although the Empire remained in some sense, it was in the guise of the Byzantine autocracy. At the same time, Christianity was spreading its faith and its diocesan structure. This much was and is dramatically obvious.

However, something else was happening. The very concept of the state, invented by the Greeks and Romans, was, admittedly temporarily, lost to view. The state is an abstract, legal entity, suited to the Greek philosophical and Roman legal minds. The medieval mind – at least until the thirteenth century – preferred to think of socio-political relationships in concrete terms, as personal connections. The prince ruled, his subjects obeyed; lords held feudal sway over vassals (see pp. 1–2).

Even so, the notion and practice of citizenship managed, very tenuously, to be sustained. This continuity was achieved partly through the agency of the Christian Church, and partly through the assertion of urban freedom or quasi-freedom from the control of the local chieftain, baron, bishop or monarch. We need, in fact, to make a distinction between the theory and practice of citizenship in the early Middle Ages. Following these preliminary remarks, we are now ready to view the relationship between citizenship and Christianity.

At first, as was vividly and gruesomely demonstrated by the episodic persecution of its adherents, Christianity was incompatible with Roman citizenship: Christians could not accept the Roman civic religion, to which a citizen had at least to pay lip-service. In course of time, nevertheless, a more tolerant atmosphere supervened, and the Christian Church expanded and was consolidated, until, in 391, Theodosius I declared Christianity to be the official religion of the Roman Empire. Now, by this time, the Empire had been divided geographically into a vast pyramidal administrative structure. One stratum of this system consisted of the *civitates*. '*Civitas*' is the Latin word for 'city', though this translation can be misleading, because in fact a *civitas* was an urban core surrounded by agricultural land and satellite towns and villages, the whole area something like the size of an English county.

When the Christian Church developed its administrative organization, it gave bishops considerable authority. Moreover – and this is what became important – they were installed in these Roman 'cities', which the Church called 'dioceses'. Consequently, civil and ecclesiastical administration coincided. And so, when the Empire collapsed, the bishops were well placed to assume political, in addition to their pastoral, leadership, bonding peasants and urban dwellers alike into a civic community with a clear identity rather akin to a Greek *polis*. Citizenship was given a new lease of life in this local sense. Then, as the cities matured, became economically vibrant, so the citizenry grew impatient of ecclesiastical authority and created their own lay civic institutions.

Indeed, Christianity and citizenship have not always been easy bedfellows because Christianity is not, in essence, a religion of this world. For this reason, in later centuries, the political thinkers Machiavelli and Rousseau notably expressed themselves quite forcibly concerning their preference for an overtly civil religion rather than the Christian Church. The fact is that citizenship evolved in antiquity when religion and politics were but two sides of the same coin, when the Olympian gods were believed to keep tutelary eyes on the city-states. Though, it is true that this tradition is mirrored in the Middle Ages through the identification by each city of its patron saint.

In one respect Christianity's view of life was markedly different from the antique beliefs that affected the concept of citizenship. The ancients held that the virtuous life was to be led in the community of one's fellows. Christianity, in contrast, taught that the temporal world was irretrievably corrupt: the good life on this earth can be only a very inadequate and approximate preparation for the good life hereafter, in the Kingdom of Heaven.

This doctrine was expounded with considerable influence by St Augustine, who was a bishop in North Africa from 396 to 430, in his magisterial work, *The City of God*. Participation in prayer rather than in civic duties was the mark of the good man.

It was not until the thirteenth century that an eminent scholar tried to manage Christianity and citizenship in association. This holy scholar was St Thomas Aquinas. Aquinas taught that all life is the expression of God's purpose. This is true of political affairs as much as any other facet of wordly life. He also regarded as a masterly analysis of that subject the *Politics* of Aristotle, whose works had recently been reintroduced into Christian Europe from Jewish and Arab sources. Thomas therefore placed Aristotle firmly in the body of his Christian model of the universe.

However, the mixture was no perfect amalgam. The effect was to undermine both a key Christian doctrine and a key feature of medieval secular political thinking. To understand the first of these consequences it is necessary to explain one of the subtleties of Aristotle's exposition of citizenship. Despite the central importance of civic virtue in the classical theory and practice of citizenship, Aristotle asserted that 'it is possible to be a good citizen without possessing the qualities of a good man' (Aristotle, 1948, 1276b). Aquinas repeated this axiom:

> It sometimes happens that someone is a good citizen who has not the quality according to which someone is also a good man, from which it follows that the quality according to whether someone is a good man or a good citizen is not the same.   (quoted, Ullmann, 1965, p. 176)

(To take an extreme example, a young Spartan in training who murdered a helot would be a good citizen, but would have offended against the Christian's Sixth Commandment.) By conceding this Aristotelean distinction, Aquinas might seem to be at variance with the principle of the absolute connection between goodness and salvation.

The second principle Aquinas undermined was the medieval comprehension of socio-political relationships. With his Commentaries on Aristotle he revived the idea of the state, which, as we have seen, had been superseded by personal authority. And so it became possible once again to conceive, not just of subjects passively submitting to their prince's commands, but of citizens actively participating in the affairs of their state. And this was a revival of a classical concept unrelated to Christian doctrine.

Classical revival

If the medieval municipal citizenship was to come to full flower, it needed three conditions to blossom. One was the full liberation of the concept from the complications and inhibitions of Christianity – after all, the condition of citizenship was devised to give individuals power over their own lives. Another condition was the strengthening of Roman law, which would give official recognition to the status. And the third condition was the releasing of cities and towns from ecclesiastical and/or secular lordly control to ensure the reality of civic freedom. In this section we shall address the first two of these requirements. The third will be surveyed in a general way in the last section of this chapter. However, the confluence of all three conditions is most clearly evident in Northern Italy in the medieval and Renaissance periods, and we shall reserve this material for separate consideration in our second section.

Aquinas was primarily a theologian and the utter commitment of 'the angelic doctor' (as he was called) to the accepted interpretation of the Christian doctrine could never be doubted. It is unthinkable, therefore, that he could consciously have wished to detach citizenship from a Christian context. This task was taken up by Marsilius (or Marsiglio) of Padua, who was born probably in 1290, 16 years after Aquinas' death. More than anyone else Marsilius restored citizenship to its secular Aristotelean interpretation.

Marsilius studied at the University of Padua, where interest in Aristotle was particularly pervasive. He gained distinction as a scholar and eventually became Rector of the University of Paris (where Aquinas had taught and written). There, perhaps in association with his assistant John of Jandun, he wrote a substantial work of political theory, *Defensor Pacis* (*Defender of Peace*). Its tone, its very purpose, indeed, was anti-papal. Three years after its publication the Pope's thunderbolts were delivered. Marsilius and John were castigated as 'the sons of Belial'. Marsilius fled to the sanctuary of the Holy Roman Emperor's court. The contrast with St Thomas could hardly be more striking.

As the title of his famous book makes manifest, Marsilius' prime purpose was to discuss international relations. Nevertheless, he takes citizenship on to his agenda. Marsilius states unequivocally that his views on this topic are derived directly from Aristotle. We have already seen in Chapter One that the Greek philosopher was adamant that the state needs no higher justification than its own existence. So Marsilius rejects any notion of citizens in their secular civic role needing guidance from God or being answerable to Him.

However, Marsilius has to diverge from Aristotle because of the difference in scale between the Greek polis and most fourteenth-century European states: he accepts the necessity for representation because the whole body of the citizenry is likely to be too large for direct participation. However, central to his discussion is his assertion and logical 'proof' that laws should derive from the will of the citizens. Here are some extracts on this point:

> The absolutely primary human authority to make or establish human laws belongs only to those men from whom alone the best laws can emerge. But these are the whole body of the citizens, or the weightier part thereof, which represents that whole body. . . a defect in some proposed law can be better noted by the greater number than by any part thereof, since every whole, or at least every corporeal whole, is greater in mass and in virtue than any part of it taken separately. . . a law made by the hearing or consent of the whole multitude. . . would be readily observed and endured by every one of the citizens, because then each would seem to have set the law upon himself, and hence would have no protest against it, but rather tolerate it with equanimity.   (quoted, Clarke, 1994, pp. 70–1)

Marsilius' argument that citizens should feel that they have a personal involvement in public affairs has a very modern ring to it. For he proposes the device of representation not just for legislation; even the holders of executive and judicial offices, he contended, should be elected. His case, moreover, is not only a statement of the nature of citizenship and what it entails; making provision for such participation is also prudent because it guarantees the stability of the state.

If Marsilius is the key medieval figure in the secularization and modernization of Aristotle's concept of citizenship, his near contemporary, Bartolus of Sassoferrato, gave a vital boost to the revivification of Roman law as an underpinning for citizenship. Bartolus was an eminent jurist, Professor of Roman Law at the University of Perugia. He reasoned that the Roman status of citizenship together with the principles of Roman law justified the idea that the people as a whole should be considered to hold the sovereign power in the state. Only when the people are sovereign can they be truly free. Like Marsilius, Bartolus makes statements that seem to pre-date very modern political thinking. Or to put it another way, there is considerable continuity from the ancient to the modern world. Again, like Marsilius, Bartolus advocated a representative system.

As Bartolus was a lawyer, it is no surprise that he wished to define who was eligible for the citizenly status. He made a distinction between citizenship by birth and by legal conferment. Nor, unlike Aristotle, did he ignore women, holding that, on marriage, a foreign wife should acquire the citizenship of her husband's state (though, admittedly, with limited privileges compared with the man's).

Thus far we have sketched the ideas on citizenship of three medieval scholars. All were Italians. For although Aquinas taught in Paris, he came from Naples, in southern Italy; Marsilius was from Padua in the north; and Bartolus, from the little town of Sassoferrato in central Italy. This was no accident, and not just because of the high standard of scholarship in Italy. Citizenship was at its most developed in that part of Europe too. Even so, it was by no means absent from the cities and towns of other west European countries.

Citizenship outside Italy

Consciousness of the classical foundations of citizenship was not confined to theory. Many a European city that had been founded by the Romans remained aware of its origins. One British historian, writing in the middle of the nineteenth century, for instance, observed: 'On the walls and gates of hoary Nürnberg the traveller still sees emblazoned the imperial eagle, with the words "Senatus populusque Norimbergenis"' (Bryce, 1968, p. 271). ('The Senate and people of Nuremberg', in imitation of the Romans' self-description as SPQR.) The example is given extra point by the fact that Nuremberg was not a Roman city! It was the done thing to boast of an ancient lineage, and for the inhabitants therefore to claim citizenship in the confines of their city.

By the eleventh century, citizenship was starting to blossom in some towns. Interestingly, as a pre-echo of Marsilius, the process started as a rejection of ecclesiastical control in the episcopal cities. It was the merchants who demanded more freedom, initially for commercial reasons. This explains why the movement started in the economically highly developed regions of northern Italy, Provence, western and southern Germany, Flanders and northern France.

By the twelfth and thirteenth centuries, town life was flourishing in Europe, enjoying and developing the twin features of urban civic life that had by then become fully established: these were a sense of community and freedom. 'Commune' is the word used to convey the first of these features. Populations were small, it must be remembered – just a few thousand (London and Paris excepted). So, the whole citizenry, as in ancient Greece, could be readily assembled for consultation or announcements. All self-respecting towns had their Town Hall, topped by a belfry for the purpose of summoning such a gathering.

But this community life would have been impossible had these towns not acquired some degree of freedom or 'immunity' from local bishop or baron or the king. The feudal context in which these struggles initially took place provided the case for a quasi-independence. By a legal fiction, towns which succeeded in their negotiations assumed the attributes of a baron, owning their own territories and exercising their own jurisdictions through their own courts.

The rights wrested from the previous overlord varied immensely from country to country and from town to town. However, they may be categorized under three headings: self-taxation; self-administration by elected magistrates and officials; and self-discipline, i.e., the maintenance of law and order by means of their own courts of law. Three further features need to be noted. One is that full citizenship, that is, the right to be involved in the election of civic officials and to be eligible for civic office, differed markedly. Secondly, the civil administration of the towns and the management of the urban economies by means of the guilds were usually intertwined, an obvious consequence of the mercantile initiative in securing urban civic freedom in the first place. The third matter to notice is that, with the development and consolidation of urban freedom and self-administration, came a sense of civic identity and pride, an essential ingredient of citizenship.

We have stressed the diversity of experiences, as many hundreds of towns achieved the status of citizenship for their inhabitants. England was perhaps the obvious example of tentative and modest citizenship arrangements, even compared with France, a similar nation-state. In France, towns declared themselves self-governing communes, and self-defending, too, through the recruitment of their own private armies. Moreover, even as late as the end of the seventeenth century some French towns were still being run rather like an ancient Greek *polis*, by a General Assembly, in a number of cases democratically, all adult male citizens participating (though Louis XIV put a stop to that). No English city or town achieved these autonomous privileges, though London briefly had ambitions along these lines.

In England effective citizenship status was acquired by means of a city or town obtaining a charter, which listed the rights and degree of independence conveyed from the king or the local lord. The years when the granting of charters was especially common were the late twelfth to early thirteenth centuries. Richard I and John were particularly generous – or desperate for the cash payments, the purchase price of a charter! Both the town as a community and certain inhabitants as individuals benefited. The individuals who had what we shall call citizens' rights and duties were described as 'citizens' if they lived in a city and 'burgesses' if they lived in a borough (the term applied to a chartered town).

The charter was, as it were, the municipality's constitution, each one different in the rights bestowed and the details listed. One notably clear charter was Lincoln's. The following very brief extracts show the kind of provisions made in these documents:

> That the commonalty shall by their common council elect a mayor from year to year of their own election. . . . And further it is provided that the commonalty with the advice of the mayor shall choose twelve fit and discreet men to be judges of the said city. . . . And there shall be no weigher of goods unless he is elected by the common council. . . . And. . . four men worthy of trust shall be elected from amongst the citizens. . . to keep an account of outgoings, tallages [taxes], and arrears belonging to the city; and that they shall have one chest and four keys. . . . Also it is provided for the keeping of the peace of our Lord the King that they that ought shall appoint two men out of each parish. . . to search their own parishes once a month. . . . Also it is provided that no foreign merchant shall remain in the city for more than 40 days for selling his merchandise. . . . And it is provided that no weaver or dyer shall dye the wool or cloths of a foreigner. (quoted, Bagley, 1965, pp. 76–7)

So, general administration, justice, police and regulation of the economy all came within the purview of the citizenry. And as to the economy, citizens would have no truck with free trade as this extract shows: tight regulations protected the city's interests against 'foreigners' – i.e. anyone from any other town. Detailed control of the town's economy was exercised by the guilds, the fraternities governing each craft or trade. The wealthy and able inhabitants – those likely to provide civic leadership – tended to be senior members of the guilds. In this way, the twin spheres of municipal life became confused through the dual roles of individual persons. Indeed, regulations tightened the overlap: in most cities and towns apprenticeship to or membership of a guild was the main criterion for obtaining full civic rights. The guilds, therefore, though strictly speaking economic and not civic institutions, came to exercise wide power over municipal affairs.

Even so, the civic area of responsibility was clear in the following two ways. First, it was the council, sitting under the chairmanship of the mayor, that made the municipal laws; and it was the borough court that exercised effective political authority and power. The court managed the taxes, administered justice and the police system and arranged the election of the borough officers. Secondly, full citizenship, that is, the franchise or freedom of the municipality, gave the individual an array of rights and duties: to elect and stand for the various offices from mayor downwards; to serve on the juries; to maintain law and order by 'keeping watch and ward', suppressing disorders; and to ensure the upkeep of the town's fabric of roads, bridges and walls.

Municipal citizenship was indeed a responsibility, even in the limited English form. But the freedom that was preserved by this responsibility made it very worthwhile, as the Italians knew and appreciated so very well.

Italian city-states

Features of citizenship

In the fullness of time many Italian towns emancipated themselves from both the overlordship of the Holy Roman Emperor and their local lay or ecclesiastical lords. They became 'communes', with their own political and judicial powers, executive authority vested in 'consuls', a title harking back to Roman times. This process was, by and large, complete by the mid-twelfth century. However, generalization about citizenship in these city-republics is difficult because evidence is patchy; also different cities had different arrangements, and the constitutional and legal conditions even in any one city changed over the years.

It is nevertheless possible to state that in the early centuries, to *c.*1100, many city-states provided a semblance of direct democracy not all that dissimilar from that of Athens in the age of Pericles. Provision was made for an assembly, called a *parlamentum*, also often termed an *arengo*, interestingly, a German word, related to 'arena'. This meeting was accorded various powers and had various compositions, differences dependent upon both the customs of the cities and political and demographic changes.

From sovereign assemblies, these gatherings declined in their range of tasks – to merely authorizing legislation and appointments, then to rubber-stamping the work of the smaller councils, which assumed the powers which they had hitherto enjoyed. Also, as the cities expanded in size, particularly in the case of the larger ones, an assemblage of all the citizens became impractical. Nevertheless, the pressure for participation was such that the councils themselves in many cities expanded in the thirteenth century. For example, in Bologna, a city of some 50,000 inhabitants, the council rose to a membership of 4,000.

Then, the process started again. Layers of participatory/representative institutions were piled up. Venice, for instance, had a small council, a commission of forty (*Quaranta*), a Senate, and a council of a thousand (*Consiglio Maggiore*). In this process, throughout Italy the *arengo* was submerged.

But in describing the institutional framework we have by-passed the question: Who were citizens? The starting-point to our answer is the clear-cut distinction that was made between rural and urban environments. As mentioned in the previous section, the 'city' of medieval city-states was the kernel of the state, encased by agricultural land and, often, very many villages. This rural area was known as the '*contadino*' (the county). Inhabitants of the *contadino* were considered yokels; only city-dwellers possessed the quality of *civilità*, civilised or civil behaviour, a term which became synonymous with '*cittadini*' (citizens).

Unsurprisingly, city-states differed in the qualifications they set for citizenship, and the distinction (or not) they made between holding the rights and duties of basic citizenship and eligibility for civic office. There was, however, one crucial requirement, namely, ownership of property in the city. An inhabitant of the *contadino* or even a foreigner could enter the ranks of the citizens by purchasing a house in the city – and therefore paying tax. Such a citizen was not necessarily required to live in that house for more than a certain proportion of the year; however, sometimes a lengthy span of residence was demanded before the status of citizen was finally conferred.

When a man became a citizen he was required to take an oath, for example, to obey the laws, to attend meetings, to pay taxes, to undertake military service. Citizens, of course, elected some of their number to the various assemblies and councils that governed the state. Direct and indirect election systems were used, also selection by lot.

Much of all this is reminiscent of Greek *poleis* in classical times, even down to the compact intimacy of the Italian communes. How Aristotle would have been delighted by this account of Pavia *c.*1330:

> they know each other so well that if anybody enquires for an address he will be told it at once, even if the person he asks lives in a quite distant part of the city; this is because they all gather together twice

a day, either in the 'court' of the commune or in the (adjoining)
cathedral piazza. (quoted, Waley, 1988, p. 29)

And, of course, as in Greek city-states, citizens would be acquainted with
each other by virtue of their service together in various civic offices.
We have already noticed the large sizes of assemblies and councils. In
addition, cities had numerous officials, though, true, not all positions
required citizen status. For example, a Siennese document of 1257
reveals the city to have 860 non-military appointments, including 90 for
tax-assessment. Such a high proportionate involvement in civic affairs
was made possible by the device of part-time employment. Furthermore,
yet another dimension to the intimacy of commune life was afforded by
membership of brotherhoods and guilds.

The integrative force of community life was often, naturally,
productive of a keen sense of patriotism. The quarrelsome relations
between the city-states occasioned many an armed conflict, which
further cemented patriotic feelings. In order to sustain and strengthen
this attitude of heart and mind, a city would construct a war-wagon
(*carroccio*), initially to lead its troops into battle, later to head civic
processions and ceremonies as a potent symbol of civic pride. The
Florentine *carroccio* was particularly noted for its splendour. In that
state a red *fleur de lis* was the symbol of the commune and a red cross,
of the people. Accordingly, the *carroccio* was decked out in red hangings
displaying these emblems, it was drawn by a pair of fine oxen, and was
accompanied by an elite bodyguard of 152 infantrymen and 48 cavalry.

Florence

Florence is, indeed, a most interesting and instructive example to take
as a case-study of Italian city-state citizenship. Founded in 59 BC as a
Roman colony on the River Arno in the Appenine foothills, it became a
wealthy mercantile city in the Middle Ages. However, no more than any
other Italian city did Florence for many centuries achieve independence
from successive overlords. It was some time in the twelfth century that
a recognizably independent government emerged. Then an executive
committee of twelve consuls came into being, governing on behalf of the
whole body of citizens, who, theoretically at least, held ultimate political
authority wielded in an assembly (*parlamentum*).

For some four centuries Florence was in effect an oligarchic republic,
governed by an upper class, though with certain democratic features
which periodically and tentatively came to the fore. The political history

of medieval and Renaissance Italy is colourful in its kaleidoscopic, often violent, changes, occasioned by foreign invasion, inter-city wars, intra-city factional and class conflicts and the seizure of power by tyrants.

Florence had its own measure of such vicissitudes – in some ways more than most other Italian cities – but managed to sustain its freedom more successfully than many. By c.1300 it was proud of this achievement, a pride made visible by the inscription of the word '*Libertas*' on the fascia of the Commune Palace. In the early 1520s Francesco Guiccardini wrote his *Dialogue on the Government of Florence*. In this work he boasts of his city's excellent record:

> despite all the tyrannies and narrow governments this city has had in the past – the ancient basis of our liberties has never been eroded; on the contrary it has been preserved as though the city has always been free: this is the citizen's equality, which is the ground absolutely most suited to receive liberty. (Guiccardini, 1994, p. 96)

Guiccardini's assertion of Florentines' equality must, however, be taken with two grains of salt. In the first place, by no means the whole populace were citizens; in the second, the political rights of the citizenry, as we shall see, fluctuated over the centuries, and more often than not there was a small upper stratum of citizens who were (to adapt George Orwell) much more equal than the others. On the first reservation, Guiccardini himself declared that 'a republic oppresses all its subjects and allows only its citizens a share in power' (Guiccardini, 1994, p. 173). In Florence, only the members of the guilds were citizens; country folk and the city plebeians were excluded from the status.

The guilds are thus the key to an understanding of Florentine citizenship, in particular, its elitist nature. The numbers are telling. Estimates suggest that c.1500 the population of the city-state was 100,000; guild membership, 5,000. By c.1200 two grades of guilds were already established: the major guilds were formed by the upper- and middle-class merchants; the minor guilds, by the craftsmen and shopkeepers. In the thirteenth century there were seven major and five minor guilds; a century later, following radical changes, the number of minor guilds was increased to fourteen.

This increase in the number of minor guilds was the work of Giano della Bella, who was also the motive force behind the Ordinances of Justice of 1293. One element of these edicts consolidated the control of the guilds over the government of Florence, which lasted in effect until 1530. In terms of citizenship, two points relating to the guilds should be noted. One is that the major guilds, except for some short periods, enjoyed more privileges and exercised more power in government appointments than the minor. The other is that even the members of the minor guilds were so jealous of their citizenly status that they helped block any attempt by the large numbers of men employed in the flourishing woollen industry from forming guilds and thus achieving the rank of citizen.

There was, in fact, nothing very simple about Florentine citizenship. To take just two examples. One concerns its electoral systems, which became a by-word for complexity, as the following instance illustrates. The leading members of the government were called priors, a majority of whom were, significantly, elected by the major guilds. In 1292 the major guilds discussed 24 different methods of electing them!

For the second example we move forward two centuries to the constitutional reforms of 1494, masterminded by the famous Dominican friar Girolamo Savanarola. One of the institutions created then was a Great Council. This was composed of all eligible (*benefiziati*) citizens. These were defined as being aged at least 29 and whose father, grandfather or great-grandfather had been selected for or had taken up one of the highest offices.

The most senior magistrate from 1293 was the Standardbearer (*Gonfalonier*) of Justice. It was he who enrolled new citizens. Foreigners and those normally resident in the *contadino* were welcomed into the ranks of the citizenry if they were willing to help reduce the city's debt. Conversely, any citizen could be stripped of his status if he failed to help the city in a crisis.

In order to forestall such shortcomings great efforts were made to instil a sense of civic belonging, loyalty and patriotism to such a degree that it would have been difficult for citizens not to have felt absorbed into the polity. We have already mentioned the potent symbol of the *carroccio*. Ceremonial, pageantry and education all played their part in sustaining this civic feeling.

In these processes the Church was especially prominent. For example, when, in the thirteenth century, Florence wished to boast that it was the 'first' of the 'Latin' cities, superior to Rome and Paris, it was an abbot who laid the corner-stone to the building bearing this message. Moreover, with great regularity, saints' days supplied the spectacle of splendid ceremonies. The Church, too, provided schools; and with the revival of Aristotelean studies, the Dominicans in Florence taught their pupils the philosopher's conviction of the naturalness of political life and the excellence of the pursuit of that style of living in a city.

Nevertheless, by the fifteenth century the republican institutions and traditions seemed under threat. Florentine citizens then, as the Dominican teachers before them, sought encouragement and lessons from the classics, in the case of these lay citizens, in the history of Sparta, Athens and republican Rome. They provided models of citizenship, and study of their experiences brought forth some great works of political literature.

Bruni and Machiavelli

Florence is indeed famous, not just as, arguably, the greatest exponent of citizenship in a city-state since the ancient Greeks; it also produced two of the greatest Renaissance writers on the subject. These were Leonardo Bruni and Niccolò Machiavelli. Each reflected in his work that immense interest in and knowledge of the ancient world that we call the Renaissance. The influence of Greece is most evident in Bruni's writing, that of Rome, in Machiavelli's. And both were proud of their city's achievements in evolving a free, citizenly form of government.

Their style of political thinking is termed 'civic humanism', that is, the belief in the vital importance of citizens' participation and of a political form of virtue drawn as a lesson from the writers of classical antiquity. Another term is 'civic republicanism', already explained in the Introduction.

Although Machiavelli's fame and influence were greater than Bruni's, it was Bruni (who lived 1369–1444) who must be credited with the typically Renaissance style of political thinking. Furthermore, he taught that citizenship was not just a subject for scholarly analysis, but required an active civic life, and that, through such participation, political improvement was possible.

Much of Bruni's writing on citizenship was undertaken to sing the praises of Florence; or, to put it another way, in singing the praises of Florence, he inevitably discussed the issue of citizenship. His most celebrated piece is his funeral oration, which he delivered on the death in battle of a leading Florentine citizen, Nanni Strozzi, in 1428. In composing this speech, Bruni explicitly modelled his message on Pericles' Funeral Oration, 1,800 years before. Like Pericles, he accords glowing praise to his own city. One of the excellent qualities of Florence, he asserts, is its constitution; and in broaching this subject, Bruni tells us a great deal about the Renaissance ideal of citizenship.

Here is an expressive passage from Bruni's Oration:

> The constitution we use for the government of the republic is designed for the liberty and equality of indeed all citizens. Since it is egalitarian in all respects, it is called a 'popular' constitution. We do not tremble

beneath the rule of one man. . . nor are we slaves to the rule of a few. Our liberty is equal for all, is limited only by the laws, and is free from the fear of men. The hope of attaining office and of raising oneself up is the same for all, provided only one put in effort and have talent and a sound and serious way of life. Virtue and probity are required of the citizens by our city. . . . And when a free people are offered this possibility of attaining offices, it is wonderful how effectively it stimulates the talents of the citizens. . . . In our city, therefore, since this hope and prospect is held out, it is not at all surprising that talent and industriousness should be conspicuous.   (quoted, Clarke, 1994, p. 78)

Notice the words 'virtue' and 'probity' in this extract. The Italian word '*virtù*' in Renaissance political discourse is very close in meaning to the Greek word '*aretē*'. Machiavelli particularly emphasized the importance of this quality. Since Machiavelli's name has been associated so strongly with the advocacy of amoral – if not downright immoral – political behaviour, one might be inclined to think his encouragement of virtue was hypocritical: the adjectives 'machiavellian' and 'virtuous' are scarcely synonymous.

However, Machiavelli's reputation must be rescued. His portrayal as a dark character derived from his cunning, ends-justify-the-means policies advocated in *The Prince*. But these policies are nothing more sinister than reflections of and reactions to the political condition of Renaissance Italy. By and large, it was a land of corruption and violence, evils from which Machiavelli personally suffered. By his age (he lived 1469–1527), even Florence was tainted, its constitution, so lauded by Bruni, under threat, as we have already described.

Machiavelli spent many years in public service, but, due to a change of regime in Florence, he was imprisoned and tortured. On his release, he retired to the exiled quiet of his Tuscan farm, where he devoted himself to writing. He wrote a history of Florence (as had Bruni before him). He also wrote a book entitled *Discourses on the First Ten Books of Titus Livy*. It was in this work, reflecting on the great qualities of ancient Rome, that he commented on the subject of citizenship.

The key feature for Machiavelli, as already indicated, was *virtù*. Packed into this concept was a variety of qualities such as loyalty, courage and the will and skill to take actions on behalf of the city in both the civilian and military spheres. And Machiavelli, partly because of the disturbed times in which he lived, laid stress on the military duties of the citizen. The military basis of Spartan citizenship may well have influenced Machiavelli; indeed, he expresses approval of Sparta for the political stability it achieved.

How were these virtues and deep sense of responsibility to be inculcated into the body of citizens? Machiavelli was hardly the sort of person to harbour any romantic ideas about the natural goodness of mankind. No: he believed in a soldier's discipline and the tenets of a civically devised religion to achieve this necessary objective. The objective of a virtuous citizenry was necessary for the most crucial of political reasons. A republic (i.e. a state based on freedom) is impossible without an active citizenry; and citizenship is impossible without a republican form of government. He held that they swam or sank together.

Let us see what Machiavelli has to say on these two matters of discipline and religion. He declared in forthright manner that 'the security of all states is based on good military discipline, and. . . where it does not exist, there can neither be good laws nor anything else that is good' (Machiavelli, 1998, p. 491). An apt religious education, he asserted, was just as vital. But it had to be of the correct kind. He claims that, whereas Christianity was not on the right track, the Romans were: their religion identified 'man's highest good. . . with magnanimity, bodily strength, and everything else that conduces to make men very bold' (Machiavelli, 1998, p. 278).

In passing, we may notice that voices have been raised in our own times in Britain, for instance, bewailing the perceived correlation between a decline in a sense of community spirit and morality on the one hand and the absence of military service for young men and the decay of religious observance on the other. No judgment is intended in this comment, just to draw the interesting parallel.

Machiavelli's views on citizenship were without doubt shaped by the times in which he lived. Even so, their validity was not confined to Renaissance Florence. When a new wave of interest in the classical world swept in in the age of the Enlightenment, his ideas enjoyed renewed relevance. In the meantime, however, political thinkers had to try to relate the concept of citizenship, based upon political freedom and equality, with the reality of sixteenth- to eighteenth-century absolute monarchy, based, contrariwise, upon the exercise of power.

The age of absolute monarchy

Problems of transition

By the time of Machiavelli's death in the early sixteenth century what are usually referred to as 'nation-states' – though they were scarcely linguistically and ethnically homogeneous – were becoming common features of the European political scene. England, France, Spain, Sweden and Poland were the large polities. They were powers to be reckoned with in their own regions, or were soon to become so. And they were answerable to no one else; they were sovereign states.

This sovereignty was personified by the monarch: the king or queen was sovereign. Moreover, the ultimate interpretation of this concept of monarchical sovereignty was absolute monarchy. No fragment of power was conceded to any other institution or group. The state was not an amalgam of citizens and magistrates as in ancient Greece and republican Rome; the state was the king: '*L'état, c'est moi*', asserted Louis XIV, contradicting the political ambitions of the *parlementaires*. Perhaps, then, absolute monarchy and citizenship were incompatible? As we shall see, the answer to this question is not simple.

For one thing, Louis XIV was something of an exception – modern monarchy did not necessarily ensure political stability. The two most consolidated sovereign states prior to *le roi soleil* suffered the most intense civil discord. From the mid-fifteenth to the mid-seventeenth century England was rent by the Wars of the Roses and the Civil War. From the mid-sixteenth century to the mid-seventeenth century France endured the period of the nine Wars of Religion and the disorders known as the Frondes. The question naturally arose as to whether some form of citizenship should be added as an ingredient to ensure the greater efficiency of the monarchical form of government.

However, the medieval practice of citizenship, which existed essentially in the small-scale municipal or city-state contexts, was either irrelevant to these emerging conditions or had to be drastically adapted. In fact, theorists (e.g. Bodin) struggled to sustain and adapt the concept, while the seeds of a new-style citizenship were germinating in small plots of fertile soil elsewhere (e.g. the English American colonies). Three problems had to be addressed.

The first of these was to translate city-citizenship into nation-state citizenship. This was, in fact, two problems in one. One was the straightforward matter of scale, namely, for Florence, think France, for example. The other was to come to terms with the fact that municipal citizenship was not in all honesty citizenship at all. A citizen of Lincoln, for instance, had little in common with a citizen of Athens precisely because Lincoln was not a state. Thus, if a man was to be a citizen of England, not Lincoln, or of France, not Lyon, that person's rights, duties and loyalty had to be transformed.

The second problem was related to that word 'loyalty'. If even the relatively mature states of England and France were still not tightly knitted into stable states, could the idea of a citizenship of the state help the process?

The third problem was the trickiest. Kingdoms have monarchs and monarchs have subjects. Indeed, to this day, Britons are, in domestic law, subjects of their monarch, as well as citizens of the United Kingdom. The question in the sixteenth and seventeenth centuries, particularly on the European continent where restraints on monarchical power were more frail than in Britain, was this: Could subjects also be citizens? If that was possible, could the additional citizenly status enhance the stability of the realm?

Three answers were forthcoming to these three problems. One solution was to correlate subjecthood and citizenship with the result that, in a monarchical state, citizenship was defined in a constrained way; and even then it really only existed in theory. The two eminent exponents of this interpretation were Jean Bodin, writing in sixteenth-century France in the shadow of the Wars of Religion, and Thomas Hobbes, writing in seventeenth-century England in the shadow of the Civil War.

The second response to the problems of this age of transition in the history of citizenship, and closely related to the first, was to accept citizenship as a proper status, but to define it as a set of duties. A conspicuous proponent of this school of thought was the seventeenth-century academic lawyer Samuel von Pufendorf, a German who lived much of his life in Sweden.

The third answer to the problems actually existed. This was to have representative institutions to reflect the people's wishes and restrain the arbitrary power of the monarch. These existed, for example, in the United Provinces (the Netherlands), Britain and Britain's North American colonies.

We shall investigate the first two responses, the theorists, in the next section, and the nature of the representative institutions in the third section.

Theorists

The most notoriously horrendous event in the series of wars in France in which Catholics were ranged against Huguenots was the Massacre of St

Bartholomew in 1572. Four years later Bodin published his *Six Books of the Commonwealth*. Bodin was a lawyer who wrote his long book with the prime objective of arguing the case for strong government, the lack of which was tearing his country apart. His book (it was a single work, though divided into sections called 'books' in the ancient manner) was the first to contain a definition of sovereignty, which he said was 'absolute and perpetual power vested in a commonwealth' (quoted, Berki, 1977, p. 125). And that power was rightfully wielded by the monarch. Despite this central concern, however, Bodin was still interested in citizenship, a topic to which he devoted two chapters.

We may extract three main elements from Bodin's views about citizenship. The first is the issue central to the theme now being considered, namely, whether subjects could be citizens. This, in fact, is not a problem for Bodin. He is quite firm:

> a citizen may be defined as a free subject dependent on the authority of another. . . . We can say then that every citizen is a subject since his liberty is limited by the sovereign power to which he owes obedience.   (quoted, Clarke, 1994, p. 87)

In truth, for Bodin, it is precisely the relationship between the subject and his sovereign that makes the former a citizen; that is,

> the mutual obligation between subject and sovereign, by which, in return for the faith and obedience rendered to him, the sovereign must do justice and give counsel, assistance, encouragement and protection to his subject.   (quoted, Clarke, 1994, p. 88)

Notice it is this connection that is crucial. We are – this is the second point to underline – a long way from Aristotle's concept of citizenship, and Bodin says so quite explicitly and unambiguously:

> It is a very grave error to suppose that no one is a citizen unless he is eligible for public office, and has a voice in the popular estates, either in a judicial or deliberative capacity. This is Aristotle's view. . . [He continues] It must. . . be emphasized that it is not the rights and privileges which he enjoys which makes a man a citizen.   (quoted, Clarke, 1994, pp. 87–8)

The third consideration Bodin stresses is the cohesive force and value of citizenship. 'The whole body of the citizens,' he wrote, '. . . constitutes a commonwealth, even if there is diversity of laws, language, customs, religion, and race' (quoted, Clarke, 1994, p. 87).

Here, then, we have a prescription for Europe in the early modern age. Citizenship underpins monarchy by being equated with subjecthood; and underpins the state by overriding lesser fissile forces.

Just as religious differences generated civil conflict in France, so they contributed to the tension between king and parliament in the reign of Charles I. In the same year that the English Civil War started, Thomas Hobbes produced his book, *De Cive* (*On the Citizen*). However, Hobbes, even more than Bodin, was insistent on firming up the principle of sovereignty. Without a strongly entrenched, absolute government, preferably a king, anarchy could supervene, a condition in which the 'life of man' would return to that suffered in the state of nature which he portrayed in his *Leviathan*: 'solitary, poor, nasty, brutish and short'. The role of the citizen is therefore obedience. For, as he asserts in *De Cive*, 'each man hath conveyed all his strength and power. . . [and] has parted with his right of resisting' (quoted, Clarke, p. 90). And then comes the give-away: 'Each citizen. . . is called the subject of him who hath the chief command.' In other words, for Hobbes, citizenship is but a word.

Our third theorist is Pufendorf, who, although a specialist in International Law, yet found time to examine the nature of citizenship. His essay on the subject, published in 1682, has a telling title: 'On the Duties of Citizens' – *duties*, not *rights*. What, in fact, we would expect at this time. Pufendorf lists the citizen's duties with exhaustive thoroughness; and the catalogue has two particular interests for us. One is that he adds the duties of the citizen to fellow citizens, not just to the state; secondly, he defines the specific duties that he considers attach to citizens in particular positions.

Quotations will clarify these two observations:

3. To the rulers a citizen owes respect, loyalty and obedience. Hence a citizen should. . . have a good and just opinion of the regime and its actions, and declare his accord.

4. A good citizen's duty towards the entire state is, to hold its welfare and safety most dear; to offer his life and property to its preservation. . . .

5. It is the duty of the citizen towards his fellows to live in friendship and peace with them, to be obliging and good-natured, to refrain from causing trouble by being petulant or difficult; to refrain from envy of the advantage of others, and not to deprive them of such advantage as they may have. (quoted, Clarke, 1994, pp. 91–2)

Points 3 and 4 are unsurprising reflections of the climate of seventeenth-century thinking that has already been sketched.

However, we should pause a while on point 5 because it is an important feature of citizenship in its fullest meaning. In Pufendorf's age it was called 'civility', and is close in meaning to Aristotle's 'concord'. In our own jargon-ridden age it is called 'horizontal' citizenship. The word 'civil', indeed, has an interesting etymology. It comes from the Latin '*civilis*', which, in turn, was derived from '*civis*', citizen. 'Civil' therefore means related to the state, and we use it in this sense in the term 'civil service', for example. In the seventeenth century it acquired the meaning of 'polite', which persists in such phrases as 'keep a civil tongue in your head'. In this sense, it has nothing to do with citizenship, though the quotation from Pufendorf shows that originally civil, polite behaviour was that which was expected of a citizen (see p. 51 above).

To conclude this survey of Pufendorf, just one example from his list of specific duties. The responsibility of the teacher will have the ring of familiarity with anyone who has been aware of the debates concerning education for citizenship at the end of the twentieth century.

> Teachers appointed to instil knowledge into the minds of the citizens should not teach that which is false or noxious: the truth should be transferred in such a way so that those listening assent not from habit, but because they have been given substantial reasons; they should not teach that which tends to disturb civil society, and hold human knowledge redundant, if it provides no gain for the life of man and citizen.   (quoted, Clarke, 1994, p. 92)

Pufendorf is not a key figure in the history of citizenship theory. Nor does his catalogue of citizenly duties relate particularly to the large nation-state – his list could well have been compiled by Machiavelli, for instance. But as a check-list it offers concise clarity not easily to be found in other writers. Nor do his injunctions specifically relate to the conditions of absolute monarchy. Yet, in a freer society than that style of polity, they would need to be balanced by a parallel list of citizens' rights. How far, we must now therefore ask, did such rights exist or were advocated in the seventeenth century?

Freedom from absolute monarchy

Although both Charles I and James II in Britain tried to install a continental-style absolutist regime, resistance in the form of the Civil War and 'Glorious' Revolution respectively blocked these attempts. The strength of English Common Law and parliamentary traditions saved

England from following the model so ready to hand in her neighbour, France. A distinction is often made – and we shall return to this in a Chapter Six – between citizens' civil and political rights. The core of the former lies in the law, and of the latter in a representative legislative assembly.

To focus on political rights in England in the seventeenth century: how far did parliament, or more particularly the House of Commons, provide Englishmen with the political rights of citizenship during this period? Basically, there was no real difference in the electoral system in the period between Edward I's 'Model Parliament' of 1295 and the Great Reform Act of 1832. Even so, although the term was scarcely used, a state political citizenship (as distinct from municipal citizenship) did exist, albeit of a most restricted kind, through this parliamentary system. Also, parliament was summoned quite frequently; indeed, Charles I's 'Eleven Years Tyranny', unconstrained by parliament, was one of the complaints that precipitated the Civil War.

Just compare the English constitutional arrangements with the French. In France the States-General was scarcely an institution for the exercise of citizenship: it had far less power than the English parliament; the Third Estate was virtually powerless against the two privileged Estates; and it did not meet between 1614 and 1789.

Furthermore, in England, the political upheavals of the Civil War and Cromwellian interregnum stimulated some lively discussion concerning the basic principle of political citizenship, namely, who should be allowed to vote. The two sides were famously expounded by senior Army officers in debates held in Putney church in 1647. Colonel Rainborough and General Ireton are the speakers in this extract.

> *Rainborough*: I think that the poorest he that is in England has a life as the greatest he. . . and I do think that the poorest man in England is not at all bound in a strict sense to that government that he has not had a voice to put himself under. . . .

> *Ireton*: That by a man's being born here he shall have a share in that power that shall dispose of the lands here, and of all things here, I do not think a sufficient ground. But I am sure if we look upon. . . what was originally the constitution of this kingdom. . . that is this: that those that choose the represeners for the making of the laws by which this state and kingdom are to be governed are. . . the persons in whom land lies, and those in corporations in whom all trading lies.   (quoted, Wootton, 1986, pp. 286–88)

So, there was a semblance of political citizenship in England in the sixteenth and seventeenth centuries, even though Ireton's restricted view reflected the practice, and was, in fact, to prevail until well into the nineteenth century.

When we turn to civil citizenship we notice a similar tentative, yet, in retrospect, hopeful scene. A series of measures in the late seventeenth century strengthened some of these rights. They included a legal ruling in 1670 which protected juries from being punished for reaching verdicts at variance with the judge's wishes. In 1679 loopholes in the operation of the right of *Habeas Corpus* were closed. And in 1689 a Toleration Act marginally reduced discrimination against Nonconformists.

Religious intolerance in seventeenth-century England was a factor in provoking the flow of immigrants to North America. The thirteen colonies, as the settlements became, soon developed their own forms of local self-government, although under the constitutional authority of the British Crown, exercised on the spot by the Governors. Nevertheless, the grip of the Governors was nowhere near as tight as that exercised by their French and Spanish counterparts in other regions of the Americas: another example of English freedom from the ambitions of absolute monarchy.

Citizenship in practice, though not in name, was exercised in various ways in the colonies; and with considerable variation from colony to colony. Each had an assembly for enacting local laws, elections being held regularly. As in the mother-country, however, the suffrage was generally restricted to men of substance, but, again, varying widely. Moreover, turn-out at elections, even of these tiny electorates, was quite feeble. Yet, one should not conclude that the colonists lacked civic consciousness. Civic participation was, instead, channelled into community activity at county and town levels.

Solid foundations were, indeed, laid down in the thirteen colonies in the seventeenth century for the vigour of citizenship in the eighteenth. Then, intellectual interest in the concept flourished, rights were strenuously asserted and duties were responsibly performed in the critical years of the American Revolution.

Only then did the word 'citizen' come tentatively into use in the English language in the sense of a member of a state, not just of a city. (In fact, this meaning did not appear in the *Encyclopaedia Britannica* until 1910!) As one American historian has said: 'In the English language the word 'citizen' in its modern sense is an Americanism' (Palmer, 1959, p. 224). To understand how this came about we need to examine eighteenth-century political thinking and the American Revolution.

CHAPTER FOUR

Age of Revolutions

Pre-revolutionary ideas

Two traditions

Emerging in England and her American colonies in the seventeenth century was a new perspective on the principle that we may identify as citizenship. What was now being spoken was the language of rights. For instance, whereas Machiavelli wrote of duties, Colonel Rainborough talked of rights. From this time forth, and particularly in the eighteenth and late twentieth centuries, two styles of thinking about citizenship have vied with each other for dominant influence. These were the civic republican and liberal versions, outlined in the Introduction of the present book.

It was Locke who placed the notion of rights firmly on the political agenda. In his *Second Treatise of Civil Government*, published in 1690, he argued that every man has the right 'to preserve. . . his life, liberty and estate' (Locke, 1962, s. 87). This formula resonated through the following hundred years to be enshrined, in adapted language, in the American Declaration of Independence (1776) and the French Declaration of the Rights of Man and the Citizen (1789). The American document has 'life, liberty and the pursuit of happiness', the French, 'liberty, property, security and resistance to oppression'. We shall look at the American and French ideas and experiences in the contexts of their revolutions in separate sections below. It is the pre-revolutionary settings that we first need to focus on here.

What, then, of Britain? In the eighteenth century her parliamentary system of government was the source of some pride. Yet it had many faults. The franchise – a basic political right of a citizen – was chaotic. From the 1760s demands were made for reform. One organization, founded in 1780, was the Society for Constitutional Information. Its statement of aims, interestingly, used the term 'citizens' in the modern sense:

To procure short parliaments, and a more equal representation of the
people, are the primary objects of the attention of this society, and
they wish to disseminate that knowledge among their countrymen,
which may. . . induce them to contend for their rights, as men, and
as citizens, with ardour and firmness.   (quoted, Dawson and Wall,
1968, p. 8)

Now, although there is strong evidence of the liberal concept of citizens'
rights gaining ground in the eighteenth century, the civic republican
ideal was also enjoying a revival almost comparable with that of the
Renaissance which has been recorded in Chapter Three. Indeed, as we
shall see later, the American and French Revolutions were fascinating
admixtures of the two traditions. We may view the civic republican
ingredient in these revolutions as the inheritance of the discussions
relating to civic virtue that preceded these dramatic political events.

In the early decades of the century there was a considerable airing
of the matter in England, for example. One of the exponents of the
civic republican principles was the politician Henry St John, Viscount
Bolingbroke. From 1726, through the extremely successful weekly
publication, *The Craftsman*, he attacked what we would today call
the sleaze of Walpole's government. He defined political virtue as 'a
disposition to oppose all instances of mal-administration' and a 'public
spirit of watchfulness over all national interests'. He urged citizens to
have a 'zeal for the constitution' (quoted, Burtt, 1992, pp. 93–4).

That great foreign admirer of the English constitution, Montesquieu,
was to write in similar vein some years later. He defined virtue not as
'zeal for the constitution' but rather 'love of the laws and of our country'
(Montesquieu, 1949, IV. 5). Montesquieu, like so many others in the
eighteenth century, both in Europe and America, was impressed by
the arguments deployed in the *Discourses* by Machiavelli, whom he
described as 'this great man' (Montesquieu, 1949, VI. 5). Rousseau, too,
had a high regard for the Florentine, writing of him as 'a good citizen'
and a 'profound political thinker' (Rousseau, 1968, p. 118n.).

Our survey of Rousseau's exposition of citizenship must, however, be
postponed for a while because it is necessary to say a few words about
the relationship between citizenship and property. We have already seen
that Locke's list of rights includes 'estate' and the French Declaration,
'property'. But the connection between property and citizenship is as old
as the status of citizenship itself. The theme is clearly audible throughout
any recitation of its history. In Greece, Spartiates were property-owners
and Aristotle insisted that property-ownership be a precondition for
citizenship. A number of arguments supported this position throughout

the centuries. Briefly: a man without property would have no leisure to involve himself in public affairs; a man with property was less likely than the man without to succumb to bribery; and the ownership of property was taken as a mark of 'virtue' in the sense of having vigorous ability.

The matter of property became a significant issue in England from the mid-seventeenth century and subsequently spread to other countries. It was raised in two forms. One was a continuation of the classical case; the other was the proper extent of the franchise. The latter will be more conveniently dealt with in Chapter Six. The classical argument concerning property focussed on the political value of landed as opposed to commercial wealth, stressing the stabilizing influence of those with a stake in the land. In its extreme form, only landowners were considered fit to have the full trappings of citizenship. Daniel Defoe voiced this opinion in England in commenting upon political rights:

> I do not place this right upon the inhabitants, but upon the Freeholders, the Freeholders are the proper owners of the Country: It is their own, and the other inhabitants are but sojourners, like lodgers in a house, and ought to be subject to such laws as the Freeholders impose upon them, or else they must remove, because the Freeholders having a right to the land, the other have no right to live there but upon sufferance. (quoted, Dickinson, 1977, pp. 88–9)

Such a sharp polarization of the population, on the other hand, ran counter to the emerging principle that a state is composed of citizens and that all citizens should enjoy a basic equality. By the middle of the eighteenth century this idea, together with the use of the word 'citizen' transformed into its modern sense, was becoming prevalent in France. One of the most persuasive exponents of this interpretation of citizenship was Rousseau.

Rousseau and citizenship

Jean-Jacques Rousseau was one of the most extraordinary phenomena in the history of European thought, extraordinary in character, in versatility and in influence. He was born in 1712 in Geneva, the place of birth being highly significant. In the eighteenth century it was a small city-republic of some 25,000 inhabitants – a kind of Greek *polis* without slaves. Of these, only about 1,500 had political rights: the top two layers – 'citizens' and 'burghers' – in a highly stratified society. Rousseau was a member of the citizen class and very proud of it: the title page of his *Social*

Contract identifies the author as 'J.-J. Rousseau, Citizen of Geneva'. Moreover, as will become clear below, he believed Geneva to be as close an approximation to his ideal state as survived in the modern corrupt world, despite its elitist citizenship system.

Rousseau spent most of his adult life in France, becoming friendly with Diderot (though the relationship did not last). In 1749 Diderot was imprisoned for his anti-religious beliefs, and Rousseau decided to make the six-mile walk to visit his friend in the castle of Vincennes. On the journey he read the newspaper *Mercure de France* in which he noticed the announcement of the Dijon essay prize on the topic: 'Has the progress of the sciences and the arts done more to corrupt morals or improve them?'

He recorded his reaction in his autobiographical *Confessions*:

> The moment I read this I beheld another universe and became another man. . . when I reached Vincennes I was in a state of agitation bordering on delirium. . . feelings rose with the most inconceivable rapidity to the level of my ideas. All my little passions were stifled by an enthusiasm for truth, liberty, and virtue.   (Rousseau, 1953, pp. 327–8)

Rousseau's life was transformed. He wrote the essay, arguing the case of the corruption of morals. He won the prize. He became famous. But not only that; he came to the self-realization that he had a unique personal insight into the decay of modern European society. He accordingly started to shift the focus of his work to social scientific analyses of these ills. His *Discourse on Political Economy* came in 1750, the *Discourse on Inequality* in 1755, and his political writing reached its zenith with the *Social Contract*, which was published in 1762.

Rousseau's ideas on citizenship are not presented, as for example Aristotle presented his, in a compact chapter or chapters; they are an integral part of his whole political thinking. In order to concentrate on the subject of citizenship, therefore, it is proposed, a little artificially, to tease out the elements under five headings. We shall reserve his views on education to a separate section; we shall end this present section with his interpretation of civic virtue, which is tightly linked to education in its broadest sense. This leaves us with liberty, equality and fraternity. By choosing these three headings we are also highlighting Rousseau's influence on the French Revolution once it was under way. For it was his most ardent disciple, Robespierre, who coined this triadic slogan to encapsulate the Revolution's objectives.

First, then, liberty. One of the most famous epigrams in political literature is Rousseau's opening sentence to Chapter One of the *Social Contract*: 'Man is born free, and he is everywhere in chains' (Rousseau, 1968, p. 49). What to do about it? Rousseau did not advocate the liberation of man by the severing of the shackles of political constraint. Man must not be loosed from the civilizing force of ordered society to return to the state of nature. Instead, he sought to define a new way of social existence that ensured the kind of civil liberty which had developed in the civic republican tradition of citizenship, rather than a liberal freedom to pursue one's own personal interests. Liberty is enjoyed and preserved by honouring one's duties in collaboration with one's fellow-citizens.

How was this to be achieved? Through Rousseau's central notion of the General Will. This is a subtle idea. In essence, Rousseau envisaged the people of a state as sovereign; as such, they collectively and freely judge what is in the community's best interests. The people are consequently in turn citizens and subjects: citizens while formulating the General Will; subjects when obeying the implications of those decisions. But in both capacities they are truly free, free from any arbitrary authority.

Nor must this participation be distorted by gross inequalities between citizens. To ensure this, Rousseau used the common device of his age of – to use current jargon – a 'virtual' social pact or contract. By living in a society individuals are bound to respect the rules of their society. So, Rousseau asserts:

> the social pact established equality among citizens in that they all pledge themselves under the same conditions and must all enjoy the same rights. Hence by the nature of the compact, every act of sovereignty. . . binds or favours all the citizens equally. (Rousseau, 1968, II. 4)

The questions naturally arise: How are these free and equal citizens to participate in defining the General Will? What fuses them into an organic whole? Following in the civic republican tradition, Rousseau believed in concord, or 'public fraternity' as he called it. And, again, in conformity with that school of thought, he believed this quality was best achieved in a small, tightly-knit community.

In his published *Letter to d'Alembert*, Rousseau declared that he was never tired of quoting Sparta. However, it was his own Geneva that was in the forefront of his mind. In his *Discourse on Inequality* he included a 'Dedication to the Republic of Geneva', where he described his ideal polity, clearly based upon his natal city. He imagined citizens making decisions in assemblies on proposals from the leaders on the most important public business... [and electing] year by year the most capable and the most upright of their fellow-citizens to administer justice and govern the state... [a republic] where the virtue of the magistrates gave such manifest evidence of the wisdom of the people that each did the other reciprocal honour. (quoted, Oldfield, 1990, p. 54)

All very well in ideal theory, but scarcely recognizable as a practical recommendation in eighteenth-century Europe. What relevance could these proposals have for a state like Poland, for instance – a huge, rambling country of some 11 million inhabitants of Protestant, Catholic and Orthodox religious persuasions and incorporating present-day Lithuania, Belarus and western Ukraine as well as Poland? A weak monarch, an irresponsible nobility and meddling neighbouring major powers reduced the country by the mid-eighteenth century from a potentially unstable polity to one of near anarchy. This parlous condition induced a worried patriot, Count Wielhorski, to appeal to Rousseau in 1771 for advice.

Rousseau's response was to adapt his city-state feeling of concord and emphasize that the Polish state was suffering from a lack of national character and therefore needed a sense of national cohesion. This could be supplied by

national institutions which form the genius, the character, the tastes, and the customs of the people, which make them what they are and not something else, and inspire that warm love of country founded on habits impossible to uproot. (quoted, Palmer, 1959, pp. 411–12)

What Rousseau was advocating was an embryonic form of nationalism. Citizenship was becoming synonymous with nationhood, a development we shall examine in Chapter Five.

National identity and allegiance differ from patriotism by the infusion of the felt need for cultural cohesion. Patriotism – loyalty and commitment to the state whatever its ethnic or cultural composition – had always been part of the package of civic republican virtue. While recognizing the new, national needs emerging in late eighteenth-century Europe, Rousseau still transmitted the traditional quality of patriotism to his readers, especially through his favourable references to Sparta and the Roman Republic. He asserted: 'Every true republican takes in with his mother's milk the love of the fatherland' (quoted, Oldfield, 1990, p. 71).

Rousseau's admiration for the ancient city-state and the civic virtue of its citizens is clear if we compare the following passage from the *Social Contract* with the excerpt from Pericles' Funeral Oration on p. 25 above.

> The better the state is constituted, the more does public business take precedence over private in the minds of the citizens. There is indeed much less private business, because the sum of the public happiness furnishes a larger proportion of each individual's happiness. . . . In a well-regulated nation every man hastens to the assemblies. . . . As soon as someone says of the business of the state – 'What does it matter to me?' – then the state must be reckoned lost.   (Rousseau, 1968, p. 140)

Rousseau and civic education

Maybe babies did imbibe patriotism from their mothers, but Rousseau was not at all confident that the effect would last without constant reinforcement throughout life. Schools, he proclaimed, must ensure that their pupils understand society's rules, the principle of equality and the sense of fraternity.

Yet, even schools, he believed, had limited efficacy in this regard. Life-long civic education (or socialization, to use the modern term) was best conducted by a state religion specifically designed for the civic purpose. Rousseau envisaged such a civil religion, not in order to pronounce and uphold tenets of theology, but to teach a creed concerning morals and duties. The discipline exacted would be fierce:

> There is thus a profession of faith which is purely civil and of which it is the sovereign's function to determine the articles, not strictly as religious dogmas, but as sentiments of sociability, without which it is impossible to be either a good citizen or a loyal subject. . . the sovereign can banish from the state anyone who does not believe [these articles of faith]; banish him not for impiety but as an antisocial being, as one unable sincerely to love law and justice, or to sacrifice, if need be, his life to his duty. If anyone, after having publicly acknowledged these same dogmas, behaves as if he does not believe in them, then let him be put to death, for he has committed the greatest crime, that of lying before the law.   (Rousseau, 1968, IV. 8)

A citizen who lies before the law is not truly free in the civic sense of living in communal freedom through the discharge of mutual duties. That freedom is paramount and is guaranteed by the General Will; therefore, in the famous assertion, 'whoever refuses to obey the general will. . . . shall be forced to be free' (Rousseau, 1968, I. 7).

The notions of citizens being taught civic virtue by a civil religion and of being disciplined to obedience to a General Will did not just remain within the theoretical pages of the *Social Contract*. Robespierre was inspired to attempt their application during the French Revolution. In contrast, Rousseau's influence on American political thinking was postponed until after the consummation of their revolution.

American Revolution

Theory into practice

Following the successful struggle against British imperial control, the thirteen American colonies were fully transformed into the new United States of America with the ratification of the Constitution in 1789. Two years later ten Amendments, known collectively as the Bill of Rights, were appended to that document in order to clarify and announce the rights of Americans. British subjects had been metamorphosed into American citizens.

It took a war to effect this transmutation. But conditions were, in any case, propitious, the conditions being a blend of tradition, experience and fashionable political theories. Consequently, the form of citizenship that emerged from the experience and opportunity of the Revolution combined continuity of colonial-age practices and the new experiment of a federal constitution, the latter being indeed a novelty for a nation the size of the USA.

The thirteen colonies had all developed their own institutions and laws yet shared attitudes which, by the mid-eighteenth century, had become cherished traditions. It must be remembered that the colonies, especially the Puritan foundations of New England, were settled by people seeking freedom. Leave aside for the moment the unhappy exception, or the gross hypocrisy, as you will, of slavery, Americans throughout their history have prized the ideal of freedom: it is epitomised by the Statue of Liberty. Also, these colonists had agreed to band together to start a new life. In 1620 the Pilgrim Fathers convened in the cabin of the Mayflower in Plymouth harbour and signed the 'Mayflower Compact', agreeing to bind themselves in a 'civil body politic'.

And so, when legal, political and economic discontents made the bonds with the mother country chafe, many colonists judged that loyalty should cede priority to the preservation of liberty and the right to contract their own form of government – even to the point of rebellion. They denied the right of a parliament at Westminster, containing not a single American, to levy new transatlantic taxes: 'No taxation without representation!' They also challenged the British constitutional principle of the sovereignty of Parliament; surely it was the people who were sovereign. It was an agenda containing the element of citizenship.

Nor were the colonists devoid of the experience of citizenship. In New England and in parts of other colonies were to be found little self-administering units akin to a Greek or medieval city-state; a township, a village really, with surrounding agricultural land. These townships were governed by a meeting of those with voting rights. They chose their officials, raised local taxes, passed parochial laws. The more southern colonies used the county as their administrative unit in a similar manner. Above these local arrangements were the colonies' governing systems. Each had an assembly with its own qualifications for franchise and membership.

Voting turn-out was low, but this was not necessarily an indicator of a low level of political consciousness. Moreover, in a small population, experience of voting and serving at township, county or assembly strata, and jury-service also, gave experience of citizenship to a fair proportion of the white male inhabitants. Awareness of political issues was much in evidence, in fact, not only during the War of Independence, but in the years immediately following too, stimulated by the French Revolution and the war between Revolutionary France and Britain.

This political consciousness found expression in the production of and interest in newspapers and pamphlets, and the drafting and ratification of state and national bills of rights and constitutions from 1776 to 1791. What were the political ideas that informed these debates and documents?

Sometimes political ideas prompt or inspire people to campaign for their promotion. Sometimes politicians succeed in putting them into practice. Sometimes political ideas are usefully – sometimes cynically – deployed to justify political actions or policies decided upon for pragmatic reasons not necessarily related to the theory. All these relationships between theory and practice can be seen at work in the American Revolution.

Much scholarly ink has been expended, some of it splashed somewhat bad-temperedly, on the question of which of the two main traditions of thinking on citizenship influenced the origins and outcome of the American Revolution. Both the civic republican ideas of Machiavelli and Locke's ideas of rights undoubtedly played their part. However, the circumstances were in fact more complicated than that. Classical philosophers and historians, Renaissance theorists, English seventeenth-century commentators on their own revolutionary period, Scottish and continental European men of the Enlightenment all contributed to the stream of American revolutionary and constitutional thought and plans.

Nevertheless, although many of the American leaders were considerable intellects – one thinks of Benjamin Franklin, Thomas Jefferson, John Adams, Alexander Hamilton, James Madison – the general run of the politically active were not academically inclined; they just wanted to liberate themselves from imperial control and create a new polity based upon their accumulated experiences of quasi-autonomy. Most of all, they needed to justify their discarding of their British allegiance – to Britain, the world and the not insubstantial number of American loyalists.

For example, Jefferson wrote two years before the Declaration of Independence the following words in denial of the authority of Parliament in London:

> Not only the principles of common sense, but the common feelings of human nature must be surrendered up, before his Majesty's subjects here, can be persuaded to believe, that they hold their political existence at the will of a British Parliament. Shall these governments [i.e. of the colonies] be dissolved, their property annihilated, and their people reduced to a state of nature, at the imperious breath of a body of men. . . in whom they never confided and over whom they have no powers of punishment or removal. . . ?   (quoted, Beloff, 1949, p. 166)

We have here the elements of the ideas of sovereignty of the people and contract. These ideas were carried through into the framing of state and national bills of rights and constitutions. The principle was adopted that the people should endorse these documents – they were contracting to live under these new rules. This understanding is illustrated most lucidly in the case of the Massachusetts constitution, which was submitted to a referendum of all free adult males. The voters were exercising their fundamental right as citizens of the new state, even though some would not qualify as political citizens for elections because of the restricted franchise then obtaining.

The most powerful and persuasive idea, however, was the concept of rights. From 1776 to 1787 the thirteen states produced their own constitutions with attendant bills of rights, which tended to be more exhaustive than the national Bill of Rights when that eventually emerged in 1791. However, what these state documents and the Declaration of Independence basically refer to are the rights of man: the Declaration of Independence asserts that 'all men are equal, that they are endowed by their Creator with certain inalienable rights' – rights given by the Creator to human beings, not by the state to citizens. None the less, these rights cannot be properly enjoyed unless the state provides consequent citizens' rights. Hence the Bill of Rights, the first Article of which is crucial:

> Congress shall make no law. . . abridging the freedom of speech, or of the press; or the right peaceably to assemble, and to petition the Government for a redress of grievances.

After all, these are the rights that form the cornerstones of citizenship in the political sense.

Franchise and legal rights

Nevertheless, one cardinal feature of political citizenship is missing from this list, namely, the right to vote. Before the Revolution all colonies had their own constitutions, which varied in the generosity of the franchise and the assiduity with which these qualifications were enforced. Concerning the latter point, a complaint was lodged in 1706 about the laxity in the conduct of elections in North Carolina, where 'all sorts of people, even servants, Negroes, Aliens, Jews and Common sailors were admitted to vote' (quoted, Kettner, 1978, p. 122).

The suffrage, unique in detail to each colony, was nevertheless in all cases pegged to specified property ownership. For example, on the eve of the Revolution the right to vote in Virginia was accorded in rural areas to men who owned 50 acres without a house or 25 acres with a house at least 12 feet square, and in towns to owners of houses of the same minimum dimensions. It is estimated that something under half the free male population qualified. In Massachusetts, with the largest proportionate electorate, the figure was over 80 per cent.

Even before the Declaration of Independence some colonies started drafting new constitutions, the Virginians leading the way, promulgating theirs on 29 June 1776. They defined their franchise very simply: 'The right of suffrage in the election for both Houses shall remain as exercised at present' (quoted, Morison, 1929, p. 153). Pennsylvania, in contrast, opted for a more democratic formula:

> Every freeman of the full age of twenty-one years, having resided in this State for the space of one whole year next before the day of

election for Representatives, and paid public taxes during that time, shall enjoy the right of an elector.   (quoted, Morison, 1929, p. 165)

In addition, non-tax-paying adult sons of freeholders also had a vote.

Evidence of this sort, indicative of an advance towards democracy, prompted considerable uneasiness, the unease made clear in the debates in the constitutional Convention called in 1787 to help frame the federal Constitution. Madison voiced his concern at these meetings, at one point asserting that

> The right of suffrage is certainly one of the fundamental articles of republican government. . . . Viewing the subject in its merits alone, the freeholders of the country would be the safest depositories of Republican liberty.   (quoted, Morison, 1929, p. 277)

The thirteen states' different definitions of suffrage for their own elections became also the arrangements for national elections. The United States Constitution did not lay down a federal franchise.

The right to vote, however, is not the only mark of political citizenship; it also involves the right to hold office. It has often been the case that stricter rules are prescribed for eligibility for political office than just for casting a vote in an election. On this matter, the federal Constitution did incorporate rulings. No one could be a member of the House of Representatives unless he was at least 25 years of age and had been legally an American citizen for at least seven years. A Senator had to be 30 years old and been an American citizen for nine years. But, strikingly, no property qualification was required for either.

Political citizenship was, therefore, restricted. Civil or legal citizenship, at least according to the Constitution, was afforded to all but the slave population. These rights were enshrined in the Fifth Amendment, which also contains the well-known right not to incriminate oneself and the concept of due process:

> No person shall be held to answer for a capital, or other infamous crime, unless on a presentment or indictment of a grand jury. . . nor shall be compelled in any criminal case to be a witness against himself, nor be deprived of life, liberty, or property, without due process of law.

By way of a footnote, as it were, we should look at the second Article of the Bill of Rights: 'A well regulated militia, being necessary to the security of a free State, the right of the people to keep and bear arms, shall not be infringed.' In the late twentieth century this became highly contentious as the hideous toll of murders by gunfire mounted while the powerfully supported National Rifle Association (NRA), on the grounds of this constitutional right, resisted attempts to restrict gun sales and ownership. But the true purpose of the Amendment lies in the first thirteen words. The right derives from the civic duty of defence of the state, harking back to the 'Minutemen' of 1776, who rapidly mobilized against perceived British oppression. It is also, crucially, part of the Revolution's inheritance of Machiavellian civic republican ideas. In the *Art of War* he wrote: 'By establishing a good and well-ordered militia, divisions [in a state] are extinguished, peace restored' (quoted, Oldfield, 1990, p. 42). This reflects our earlier comment about the twin traditions of civic thinking as contributions to the American Revolution, and is so close to the wording of the second Amendment.

Particular American issues

In the context of prevailing political ideas and the circumstance of the Americans' creation of a brand new state, it was inevitable that they should have drawn up guidelines for the franchise and a list of rights. When the French changed their regime in 1789 they followed suit. However, the American Union was faced with three major issues relating to citizenship which were at that time peculiar to itself.

First, there was the question of naturalization. Americans knew themselves to be a nation of immigrants. (The Native Americans, notoriously, 'did not count', except as an inconvenience eventually to be disposed of.) The thirteen states covered a substantial area, sparsely populated. The first census, conducted in 1790, revealed a population of just under 3.9 million, 700,000 of whom were blacks, mainly slaves. This compared with a population of the very much smaller England and Wales in 1801 of nearly 9.2 million. New American citizens were needed, so naturalization regulations were vital.

The second issue was the federal system of government. How could individuals be simultaneously citizens at both levels, state and national? The only precedents, the United Provinces and Switzerland were much smaller and provided few lessons.

The third particular issue was slavery. No other state that professed to be a modern society had internal slavery (that is, excluding the cases of colonies), let alone such a huge proportion of its population subjected to that condition. What honesty could there be in the concept of a state composed of free and equal citizens if over one-sixth of the population was excluded?

We conclude this section with a brief examination of the first of these issues. The second and third are included in appropriate places in Chapter Five. For, in truth, the Founding Fathers ignored both of these problems. Future generations had to cope.

To return now, therefore, to the pre-revolutionary era and the question of naturalization. The colonies had need of immigrants – for economic development, for labour, for defence against the Native Americans and, until the cession of the French colonies in 1763, against those enemies. English regulations on naturalization were tighter than the colonies would have wished. Some, especially in New England, accommodated their needs in two ways. One was to treat aliens as if they were British subjects. For example, in 1641 Massachusetts permitted aliens to attend town meetings to 'move any lawfull, seasonable, and materiall question, or to present any necessary motion, complaint, petition, Bill or information' (quoted, Kettner, 1978, p. 111). The other way of dodging English regulations was for colonial Assemblies to pass their own Acts. In 1773 the British government banned such impertinent procedures, much to the colonists' anger.

And so, when the colonies achieved independence, they set about defining their own laws. These varied in detail and the stringency of control, but basically the states required an oath of allegiance and a period of residence either for admission to citizenship or, at least, for the full enjoyment of political rights. Also, the federal Constitution, as we have already seen, laid down residence qualifications for members of Congress. It also declared that 'The Congress shall have the power. . . . To establish an uniform rule of naturalization' (Article 1.8).

The need to tidy up the confused situation in this transition period was made manifest by the election to the Senate in 1793 of a certain Albert Gallatin. He had migrated from Switzerland in 1780, taken oaths of allegiance and bought land in both Massachusetts and Virginia, and fought in the War of Independence. Yet, his qualification as a citizen was challenged on the grounds that his acceptance by Virginia was technically invalid. He was deprived of his seat in 1794. The following year Congress passed an Act to establish federal control of naturalization. The states gradually fell into line.

News of the American Revolution – the war and the constitutional changes – made a dramatic impact on Europe, especially France, which had provided signal military support to the Americans. In 1789 the young French playwright Marie-Joseph Chénier staged his *Charles IX*, audaciously and bitterly criticizing Church and monarchy. Audiences received it frenziedly. It contained the following lines:

> This vast continent that the seas surround
> Will soon change Europe and the world.
> There arise for us, in the fields of America,
> New interests and a new system of politics.
> (quoted and trans., Palmer, 1959, p. 506)

But, by then, the French had already plunged into their own attempts at defining citizenship.

French Revolution

Consciousness of citizenship

Commenting on the influence of the American Revolution, Tocqueville wrote that 'the French saw in it a brilliant confirmation of theories already familiar to them'. He found evidence, for instance, that on the eve of their own Revolution even French peasants were referring to their neighbours as 'fellow citizens' (Tocqueville, 1955, pp. 146–7). The concept of a national citizenship was already abroad before 1789; and then it became the salient characteristic of the Revolution, symbolized by the dramatic decision of the National Assembly in June 1790 to abolish titles of social rank: henceforth all were *citoyens/citoyennes*. (Though, in truth, the appellation was widely used only briefly in the heightened political atmosphere of 1793–94.)

However, we run ahead of ourselves; we must return to the year 1789, so packed with significant events. The royal government, desperate for funds, was forced to the expedient of reviving the long discarded States-General. In order to allow the representatives to speak for each of the three Estates, provision was made for the electorate to draw up lists of grievances (*cahiers de doléance*). These documents, an extraordinarily rich source of evidence about ideas, opinions and problems of the time, reveal a widespread consciousness of the notion of citizenship, cutting across the divisions between the constituted orders.

The rights asked for were mainly of the legal kind, which came to be enshrined in the Declaration of the Rights of Man and Citizen. Two topics, however, require separate mention. The first is an interesting reflection of the civic republican tradition that the citizen has a duty to perform military service. One *cahier* entry, for instance, reads: 'Every citizen is a soldier in time of need' (quoted, Hyslop, 1934, p. 121). The second topic to note is a common stress on the need for a national system of schooling with provision for civic education. To take one *cahier* of the nobility as an example: this urged the teaching of

> a patriotic catechism, which will explain in a simple and elementary manner the obligations of a citizen, and the rights which derive from the obligations. . . obedience to the magistrates, devotion to the *patrie*, and to the king.   (quoted, Hyslop, 1934, p. 180)

The *cahiers* provided something like an agenda for the States-General.

That body having assembled, then its reformist members having transformed themselves into a National Constituent Assembly, urgent work began on the drafting of a new, written constitution, to be prefaced by a Declaration of Rights. What were these rights? Who were to enjoy them? Who were to elect the new Assembly under the new Constitution? Who were to be eligible to serve as representatives? All these were questions about citizenship.

The Declaration of Rights proclaimed basic civil rights such as equality before the law, freedom from arbitrary arrest and freedom of speech. Following on, the lengthy Chapter V of the Constitution spelt out legal safeguards for the citizen in the face of the judicial system. The Constitution also defined in some detail who were French citizens, how foreigners could become naturalized and how the status of citizen could be lost.

Not that the final wording was easily agreed, though the provision of civil rights provoked less controversy than political rights. Generalized legal definitions of citizens were easily accepted; whether certain categories should be excepted did, however, occasion debate.

How could any exceptions be condoned when the Declaration of the Rights of Man and Citizen incorporated forthright statements suggesting that distinctions were incompatible with basic principles? The first article boldly and plainly asserts that 'Men are born, and always continue, free, and equal in respect of their rights'. The third article declares that 'The nation is the source of all sovereignty'. And the sixth states: 'The law is an expression of the will of the community. All citizens have a right to concur, either personally, or by their representatives, in its formation'. What, then, could be the definition of citizenship and how could the ownership of rights be *construed* when the key words 'equal' and 'nation' and 'will of the community' were enshrined in the fundamental document?

Virtually nowhere were slaves, Jews or women accorded political rights. Yet the possibility of their inclusion, as well as other doubtful categories, was discussed in France, as will now be outlined, though the issues of the rights and role of women is a matter more conveniently addressed in Chapter Six.

The question of the status of blacks, free as well as slave, was forced to the attention of politicians in Paris by conditions in the Caribbean colonies, especially Haiti, which were thrown into turmoil by talk of equality in the metropolitan country. Not surprisingly, successive French governments vacillated on this problem. The main religious minorities were given civic rights – the Huguenots after much acrimonious debate, and Jews, on condition that they swore the civic oath of allegiance. And there was yet another category of men about whom there were doubts, namely, those who pursued what many considered to be the infamous professions of public executioners and actors! Even they were given the benefit of the doubt and the vote.

All these discussions, heated and prolonged as some of them became, were, for practical purposes, peripheral to the central question of the aptness of imposing property or wealth qualifications as a precondition for political rights. The two most distinguished political thinkers of the French Revolution were ranged in these crucial debates against each other; Sieyes in favour of qualifications, Robespierre against.

Sieyes and Robespierre

The Abbé Sieyes was born in 1748 and died in 1836, thus spanning the *ancien régime*, Revolution, Napoleon, Restoration, 1830 Revolution and the early years of the Orleanist monarchy. In addition to his writings on politics he had a distinguished career of political activity; though, true, when asked what he did during the period of the Terror in the regime of the Committee of Public Safety, he gave the celebrated reply: '*J'ai vécu*' ('I lived'). Sieyes is credited with over thirty published works, mostly quite brief, the most famous of which – indeed, the most famous of all the political writings to emerge from the French Revolution – was *Qu'est-ce que le Tiers État? (What is the Third Estate?)*. He produced this pamphlet anonymously in January 1789. It attacked privilege with considerable vigour. It had a resounding impact.

In July 1789 Sieyes published his thoughts on the rights of man and the citizen. Here we find a passage crucial to his conception of citizenship and to the debate on the political rights of citizenship in the early phase of the Revolution. He expounded a basic distinction between natural and civil rights on the one hand and political rights on the other:

> It would be better, for the sake of linguistic clarity, to call the first
> passive rights, and the second active rights. All the inhabitants of a
> country ought to enjoy within it the passive rights of a citizen; all
> have a right to the protection of their person, of their property, of their
> liberty, etc.; but all do not have a right to take an active part in the
> formation of public powers: not all are active citizens. . . those who
> contribute nothing to the support of the public establishment, ought
> not to exercise an active influence on the public weal. (quoted,
> Forsyth, 1987, pp. 117–18)

Sieyes, reluctantly, deposited all women in the passive category because
of public hostility to their enfranchisement. And he reckoned that about a
quarter of adult French males lacked the qualities to be given the vote.

Sieyes' proposition of active and passive citizenship was more than
theoretical musing. The National Assembly had to decide on the question
of the franchise in order to inscribe the regulations in the Constitution.
Most members accepted Sieyes' division as highly sensible and drew the
distinction that an active citizen should be he who paid the equivalent of
three days' unskilled work in direct taxes.

However, discrimination by wealth did not stop there, and for two
reasons. One derived from the device of two-tier indirect elections.
Active citizens elected electors; and these latter were defined as those
paying at least the value of ten days' work in direct taxes. The other
reason was the qualification to be a deputy. This was proposed as the tax
equivalent of fifty days' wages, translated in monetary terms as a *marc
d'argent* (silver mark).

Elections were conducted on the basis of the 1789 Constitution in
1791. It was then calculated that 4,298,360 men (and they had to be over
25 years of age) qualified as active citizens. The total population was
probably something under 26 million. In comparison with England and
the American states at this time, this was not an unreasonable proportion.
But it was scarcely democractic. Before those elections were held for the
new Legislative Assembly a few deputies in the National Assembly did
argue the democratic case. The most notable of these was Robespierre.

Maximilien Robespierre was born in 1758 in Arras, practised as a
lawyer, entered politics in 1789, and became the leading light in the
Jacobin Club and, briefly, of the Committee of Public Safety. He was to
epitomize the Revolution by devising the slogan 'liberty, equality and
fraternity'; by his deep commitment to Rousseau's concept of the General
Will and ideal of civic virtue; and, horrifically, by his association with
the policy of Terror, to which, by the ironic twist of factional politics and
frightened reaction, he himself fell victim.

Robespierre's democratic convictions were evident at the very beginning of the Revolution. Having been invited by the clog-makers of Arras to write their *cahier* for them, he attacked the discriminatory attitude of the municipal authorities towards the poor, 'precisely those most entitled to protection, concern and respect' (quoted, Hampson, 1974, p. 38).

It is no surprise, therefore, that, later that year, as a deputy, he spoke trenchantly in the Assembly against the franchise restrictions. He argued that the distinction between active and passive citizens contradicted the equality so proudly pronounced in the Declaration of Rights. He carefully explained:

> Each individual therefore has the right to participate in making the law which governs him and in the administration of the public good which is his own. If not, it is not true that all men are equal in rights, that every man is a citizen. If he who only pays a tax equivalent to a day of work has fewer rights than he who pays the equivalent to three days of work. . . then he who enjoys 100,000 livres of revenue has 100 times the rights as he who only has 1,000 livres of revenue.   (quoted, Hunt, 1996, p. 83)

And he returned to the attack in April 1791:

> It is not taxes that make us citizens: citizenship merely obliges a man to contribute to public expenditure in proportion to his means. You may give the citizens new laws, but you may not deprive them of their citizenship. The upholders of the system that I am denouncing have themselves realized this truth; for, not daring to challenge the title of citizen in those whom they condemn to disinheritance, they have confined themselves to destroying the principle of equality inherent in that title by drawing a distinction betwen active and passive citizens.   (quoted, Clarke, 1994, p. 114)

Despite his forensic and logical skills, however, Robespierre failed in his efforts to democratize the system of voting. He also campaigned against the *marc d'argent* qualificaton for candidates. In taking that position he had allies (even Sieyes seems not to have supported such a prescription); and the Constitution emerged as requiring only that those standing for election should be active citizens. None the less, it was an empty victory because the electoral arrangements for the new Legislative Assembly were already under way before this change could be put into effect.

Nor was this the only discrepancy between constitutional intention and electoral practice. Giving active citizenship status by the test of taxation was not very practicable, not least because of variations in wage levels; moreover, response to the 1791 election was widespread apathy among the stratum of citizens thus designated.

Even so, the story of citizenship during the French Revolution is by no means typified by the poor turn-out in this national election. What is much more characteristic is local civic activity, especially in the highly politicized capital-city and in the shaping of Jacobin ideology.

The development of citizenship

If parts of citizenship may be equated with the expression of views about public affairs and organization of the citizenry to achieve change, then French men and women forcefully acted out their citizenly roles in transforming municipal government in thousands of towns, and in the violent dramas of the journées, the periodic uprisings in Paris.

Resentment against the oligarchical municipal corporations and central government's interference in town affairs became widespread in the spring of 1789. Moves to reform these obsolete systems of local administration were accelerated and radicalized by the unbelievable success of the Parisians in securing the surrender of the Bastille on 14 July. Renovation of provincial municipal government took various forms, in some towns being effected by violence in order to expel the oligarchs from power and erect more democratic authorities.

In December a law rubber-stamped the municipal revolution of the shopkeeper and artisan citizens. Furthermore, in true civic republican style these new elected town councils created their own militias and proudly boasted their new civic identity and autonomy.

Meanwhile, the citizens of Paris were assuming control of their own affairs. For the purposes of electing representatives to the States-General, the city had been divided into 60 Districts. After the election the electors – there were 400 of them – continued to meet, effectively displacing the ancien régime authorities. Following the fall of the Bastille, these Districts formally created an elected Commune of 120 members. They also formed their own militia, of 12,000 men, which inaugurated the National Guard citizen army. Then, in 1790, Paris was re-divided into 48 Sections. Each of these thereafter handled its own affairs by a mass meeting of all its active citizens (on average about 17,000), numerous specialist committees, and its own magistrates' court. These Sections played decisive roles in the turbulent events in the city from 1792 to 1794.

In his fine novel, *Les dieux ont soifs* (translated in the Penguin edition as *The Gods Will Have Blood*), Anatole France creates, through the character of Évariste Gamelin, a most evocative word-picture of the Paris of the Sections. The scene is set in April 1793 on the eve of the purging of 'Girondin' deputies of the Convention by the dominant Jacobin Mountain. The following extract is drawn from the opening pages:

> Very early one morning, Évariste Gamelin, artist, pupil of David, member of the Section du Pont-Neuf. . . was to be seen approaching the ancient church of the Barnabites, which had served for three years, since 21st May, 1790, as the meeting-place for the general assembly of the Section.
>
> the arches [of the nave were now used by] the red-capped patriots gather[ing] to elect the municipal magistrates and to discuss the daily affairs of the Section. . . . The tablet of the Rights of Man stood on the plundered altar.
>
> In this nave on two evenings each week the public meetings were held, from five o'clock until eleven o'clock. . . . For the women and children who came to these gatherings in quite large numbers, rose a high, rough-planked platform.
>
> On this particular morning there was seated at his desk. . . one of the twelve members of the Committee of Surveillance. . . .
>
> Évariste Gamelin picked up the pen and signed the petition against the 'Girondins'. The working-class magistrate said,
>
> 'I knew you'd come and put your name to it, Citizen Gamelin. Made of the right stuff, you are. That's the trouble with this Section. . . . Lukewarm most of them. No moral backbone'. (France, 1979, p. 27)

Gamelin was a man of civic virtue in the dedicated Jacobin sense.

The feeling of being a citizen was sedulously fostered throughout France and throughout the Revolution by civic ceremonies, such as the planting of 'trees of liberty'. The most extraordinary spectacle occurred in Paris on the first anniversary of the fall of the Bastille, when over a quarter of a million converged on the capital to witness a huge theatrical celebration on the *Champs de Mars*.

France in the early 1790s was becoming increasingly democratic in intention and in practice. When, after the deposition of Louis XVI, the Convention set about framing a new, republican Constitution, a number of differences from its predecessor were clearly evident. In the matter of citizenship, crucially, the distinction between active and passive citizens was abolished, a decision underlined by the statement that 'The sovereign people is the totality of French citizens'.

In addition, there is a glimpse of the concept of what we would now call a welfare state, or social citizenship. Thus Article 21 of the Declaration of Rights reads:

> Public assistance is a sacred duty. Society owes its less fortunate citizens subsistence, either by providing them with work, or by ensuring the means of existence for those who have no work.

This Constitution was never put into operation: its interest is therefore as a mirror of the dominant political thinking – Jacobin thinking, as voiced in the Jacobin clubs. The politicians of the successive representative assemblies from 1789 founded clubs where the like-minded could meet. Politically literate and enthusiastic citizens also joined. Moreover, this Parisian practice was replicated in provincial towns. The most influential and energetic were the Jacobin clubs. The mother society in Paris met in the Rue St Honoré monastery of the Dominican monks, nicknamed 'Jacobins', hence the name of the political club.

A reasonable estimate of the total membership of Jacobin clubs in their heyday in 1793 is about half a million, spread over roughly 6,000 clubs. The active members were the truly active citizens of the Revolution in the sense of civic participation by choice, not Sieyes' definition by supposed competence. Social composition was a cross-section of the working- and middle-classes. Moreover, those Jacobins who were utterly committed to the ideals of the Revolution, who participated in local affairs, notably in running the Paris Sections, came to think of themselves as an elite, the true, civically virtuous patriots.

No Jacobin was more determined to lay stress on the vital need for civic virtue than Robespierre. Yet, this conviction led him and those of like mind into a decidedly unfortunate interpretation of citizenship. For the Jacobin zealots, citizenship had to be placed at the very heart of an individual's life; family, regional attachment, Christianity – all had to be sacrificed to the civic purpose. Unhappily for Robespierre his simple Rousseauist belief in the natural goodness of the people was confronted, particularly in the perilously critical months of 1793–94, by so much evidence, in his mind, of human wickedness.

How to explain this contradiction? Robespierre argued that there were both the politically righteous, who were true citizens, and the politically iniquitous, who were false to the title of citizen. He declared:

There are two kinds of people in France, one is the mass of citizens, pure, simple, thirsty for justice and friends of liberty. These are virtuous people who spill their blood in order to lay the foundations of liberty. . . . The others are a seditious, intriguing rabble. . . rogues, foreigners, hypocritical counter-revolutionaries.
(quoted [in French], Cobban, 1968, p. 187)

Those wanting in civic virtue had to be forcefully encouraged to a true citizenship – Robespierre's model was the Lycurgan regime in Ancient Sparta – or the fatherland be cleansed of their dangerously corrupting presence through the operation of the guillotine: in short, the policy of Terror. For virtue and terror, he came to believe, were symbiotically linked: 'virtue without which terror is squalidly repressive, terror without which virtue lies disarmed' (quoted, Rudé, 1975, p. 118).

The concept of citizenship had come to a dreadful pass if the Greek ideals of an elite of equals and of civic virtue could be upheld in the so-different context of a large nation-state only through an atmosphere of terrible fear, imposed by a cadre of self-defined virtuous men.

CHAPTER FIVE

Modern and Contemporary Themes I

Nationality and multiculturalism

Pre-nineteenth century

After the French Revolution, according to the distinguished British political scientist Graham Wallas, European statesmen thought that

> no citizen can imagine his state or make it the object of his political affection unless he believes in the existence of a national type to which the individual inhabitants of the state are assimilated; and he cannot continue to believe in the existence of such a type unless in fact his fellow citizens are like each other and like himself in certain important respects.   (quoted, Oommen, 1997, p. 135)

It is instructive to compare this quotation with another, by the notable German sociologist Jürgen Habermas, who has crisply asserted that 'Citizenship was never conceptually tied to national identity' (Habermas, 1994, p. 23).

Before the eighteenth century, certainly, citizenship and nationhood could scarcely have been related because they were linked to different socio-political entities. To take three examples. Citizens of ancient Greek *poleis* owed their civic status and were tightly bonded to their particular city, to the extent of often bitterly warring against rival cities. Yet this did not preclude a sense of 'Greekness', defined most famously by Herodotus as 'the common blood, the common language; the temples and religious ritual; the whole way of life we understand and share together' (Herodotus, 1954, p. 550). Roman citizens lived throughout the whole wide expanse of the Empire without necessarily divesting themselves of their own ethnic cultures. And in the Middle Ages, citizenship adhered to municipalities, not countries or ethnically identifiable regions.

These are fairly clear-cut examples. However, when we come to the eighteenth century, semantic confusion prevents a straightforward resolution of the apparent contradiction between the quotations from our two scholarly authorities.

Until the eighteenth century the word 'nation' had different connotations from those associated with it today. Then it started to become synonymous with 'country' or 'fatherland', and the people who inhabited it. So, just as the word 'citizen' was being detached from its municipal meaning and attached to the state, so the term 'nation' was also becoming attached to the state. This is by no means to say that they necessarily had exactly the same meanings in the eighteenth century, because there were complications. The question was still to be resolved: Was a nation to be defined by political or by cultural criteria?

If political, then, in a reasonably democratic state, the two terms would approach synonymity. This happened in the French Revolution. The Abbé Sieyes provided the theoretical statements. 'What is a Nation?', he asked; and gave the answer: 'A body of associates living under *common laws* and represented by the same *legislative assembly*, etc.' (Sieyès, 1963, p. 58). Not a bad approximate definition of citizens in civil and political senses. This alignment of nationhood and citizenship also appeared in the Declaration of Rights, which specified that 'sovereignty resides essentially in the nation', and continued, 'The law is the expression of the general will'.

Furthermore, the Constitution of 1791 offered the opportunity of French citizenship to foreigners, thus signalling the absence of any necessary connection between the civic status and nationality in the cultural, ethnic or racial senses. The list of those who were deemed to be French citizens included: 'Those who, born in France, of a foreign father, are permanently resident in the kingdom.' And 'Those who, born outside the kingdom of foreign parents, resident in France, become French citizens after five years continuous domicile in the kingdom' if they meet certain conditions indicative of this commitment to France. Indeed, we may interpret the emergence in the eighteenth century in some states, notably Britain and France, of a sense, expectation even, of national loyalty, as being a transmutation in the new environment of a modern nationalist political culture of the old civic republican virtue of patriotism.

Nineteenth century

In practice, France did not become the model for openness to national citizenship. Massive immigration into the United States established that country as the exemplar. Between 1820 and 1865 five million arrived; between 1870 and 1920, nearly 20 million. Assimilation into the ranks of American citizens, however, usually required the civic political test of knowledge of the Constitution and the functional test of literacy.

The ability to read and write, needless to say, presupposed a certain basic command of the language. But if citizenship requires an understanding of the language of the nation-state, the nineteenth-century concept of nationhood/nationalism was also usually understood to have a linguistic basis. The tying together of political citizenship and nationality through the medium of a common tongue was classically expounded by John Stuart Mill. He declared that

> Free institutions are next impossible in a country made up of different nationalities. Among a people without fellow-feeling, especially if they read and speak different languages, the united public opinion necessary to the working of representative government cannot exist. (Mill, 1910, p. 364)

Yet in three major European countries – not to mention a host of lesser examples – this conjunction of citizenship and linguistic nationality barely existed when Mill wrote these words.

To take Italy, first and briefly. Mazzini envisioned the national unification of the peninsula by the will of 'all the citizens that Italy contains' (Mazzini, 1961, p.236). Yet, when that unification came about (from 1859 to 1870), it is estimated that only 2 per cent of the population could speak Italian.

Even in France, that quintessential European nation-state, it is reckoned that in 1789 half the population could not speak French at all. This was worrying. In 1794 Barère, member of the Committee of Public Safety, voiced this concern;

> Citizens! the language of a free people ought to be one and the same for all. . . . We have observed that the dialect called Bas-Breton, the Basque dialect, and the German and Italian languages have perpetuated the reign of fanaticism and superstition. . . prevented the Revolution from penetrating nine Departments, and favoured the enemies of France. . . take away the empire of priests by teaching the French language. . . . It is treason to the fatherland to leave the citizens in ignorance of the national language. (quoted, Macartney, 1934, pp. 110–11)

However, as late as 1870, this Jacobin ideal of a France unified by a common language and by its means a common national identity had still not converted millions of peasants from their tight, medieval attachment to their village and local tongue. These rural dwellers were legally citizens; some even had the vote (about five million at the time of the 1876 election). Yet it is a frail kind of citizenship when the citizen has so little of what Mill called 'fellow-feeling' and feels so little connection with his nation-state. During the 1880s the French state strove, by education and military service, to 'nationalize' all its citizens. It is said that some schools in Rennes posted notices commanding, 'It is forbidden to spit and speak Breton'!

At the same time, the new German Empire was pursuing its policy of Germanization with its Polish-, French- and Danish-speaking populations. Yet, even if these people round the rim of Germany learned the language, they were not considered 'real' Germans. They were not members of the *Volk*. In contrast with, for example, the USA, Britain and France in the nineteenth century, where legal citizenship was considered virtually identical to nationality (however defined), in Germany that fusion was hindered by two factors. One was the disunited condition of the country until 1871; the other was the concept of the *Volk*.

In 1807–8 Fichte, in his *Addresses to the German Nation*, attempted to relate German nationality to state citizenship, arguing that the more an individual loved the German fatherland, the better citizen he would be of his own particular state. But, already, the notion of the *Volk* was emerging: the idea of a people clustered together by a natural common 'essence' – in its purest form, the Germans. This belief, that nationhood is *völkisch*, means that a person is born with a nationality, it cannot be conferred; it is in the 'blood', not a legal status.

In contradistinction to the French post-1789 tradition, therefore, German citizenship and cultural nationhood became much more tightly bonded, in effect, fused. This interpretation was cemented into German law in 1913 by according the perpetual right of German citizenship to all 'Germans' in whatever country they might be residing.

Twentieth century

The concept of the *Volk* was in origin the product of the Romantic movement. It became coarsened in the Nazi doctrine of *Blut und Boden* (blood and soil), which was taken to justify the primarily anti-Semitic Reich Citizenship Law of 1935 and its terrible aftermath. Article 2 included this definition:

A citizen of the Reich may be only that subject who is of German or kindred blood, and who, through his behaviour, shows that he is both desirous and personally fit to serve loyally the German people and the Reich.   (quoted, Snyder, 1962, p. 163)

Denial of the rights of citizenship by the criterion of race was not confined to the Third Reich. The subjection of black people under the apartheid regime in South Africa and in the southern states of the USA provide two other obvious examples.

In 1910 Britain created the Union of South Africa with its own federal Parliament. Only whites were allowed to participate in the political process. However, since no other black Africans in other colonies had political rights at this time, their non-enfranchisement in South Africa was hardly surprising. What made South Africa unique in the continent was the steady stripping away of any civil rights which the majority black population might have expected to enjoy.

By creating the legal device that the black 70 per cent of the population were properly citizens of the 13.5 per cent of the land designated as their 'homelands' or 'Bantustans', the Afrikaner-controlled government of the Union, later Republic of South Africa, from c.1950 could claim some kind of twisted consistency in abridging the blacks' rights in the bulk of the state. Furthermore, the style of enforcement of the system ensured that this denial of rights was draconian. A UN report spoke of 'The weaponry of terror, deployed under the sanction of law' (Friedman, 1978, p. 39).

Not until the promulgation of the new post-apartheid Constitution in 1996 did South Africa become a multi-racial 'nation' of legally equal citizens. Article 1.3 asserts:

(1) There is a common South African citizenship.

(2) All citizens are –
  (a) equally entitled to the rights, privileges and benefits of citizenship; and
  (b) equally subject to the duties and responsibilities of citizenship.

But at least South African blacks were not slaves, as some four million American blacks were at the time of emancipation in the 1860s. The Thirteenth Amendment to the Constitution, abolishing slavery, was followed three years later, in 1865, by the Fourteenth, which confirmed that,

All persons born or naturalized in the United States, and subject to the jurisdiction thereof, are citizens of the United States and of the States wherein they reside. No State shall make or enforce any law which shall abridge the privileges or immunities of citizens of the United States.

Citizens in law they may have been; but many devices, from lynch-mobs to 'Jim Crow' laws of segregation, ensured for at least another century that blacks, particularly in the Deep South, were, at best, 'second-class' citizens – a term coined by the politician Wendell Wilkie in 1944 in condemnation of this practical discrimination. Steadily, often against grim white hostility and obstruction, blacks proved their civic consciousness by organizing their own protests against the inequality from which they suffered. And gradually they became something like full citizens: for example, by registering to exercise their political right to vote; by demanding and securing their civil right to effective and fair justice; by demonstrating for their social rights against 'petty apartheid' (to use the South African term) and achieving desegregation on buses and in restaurants; and by pressing for, and at least partially winning, economic and employment levels more comparable with those of white Americans.

The sufferings of the American blacks were bitter commentary on the equality, life, liberty and pursuit of happiness proclaimed in the Declaration of Independence as Americans' birthrights. Moreover, if the condition of the coloured people was a blatant contradiction of the eighteenth-century proposition that all men are created equal, it was also, after Emancipation, a contradiction of the supposed principle that all citizens are of equal status. But this putative essence of the civic ideal has been so often breached that a speedy transition from slavery to complete citizenship could hardly have been expected.

Yet, although their origins in slavery and their readily identifiable skin pigmentation delayed the incorporation of blacks into a homogeneous American civil society, at least they did not meet the barriers of different religions or languages. The language issue has nevertheless been a problem for other people in the United States. Nineteenth-century immigrants from Europe and Asia acquired citizenship by learning English; and government policy succeeded in expunging many of the 'barbaric tongues' of the Native Americans (who, incidentally, were denied citizenship until 1924). However, the issue of the great numbers of Spanish-speaking citizens has raised the question as to whether the USA is becoming a bilingual country.

The late twentieth century was an era of heightened ethnic consciousness and sensitivity in all continents. Demands for rights and/or the institutionalization of separate cultural identities exerted great strains on many a so-called 'nation-state'. Discontent was sometimes directed at a government as the instrument of oppression or homogenization, sometimes between component peoples of the state who felt unable to live peaceably side-by-side. Devolution, as in Spain and Great Britain, for example, is a civilized compromise; periodic Tutsi–Hutu slaughter in Burundi and Rwanda is an example of the collapse of all civilized values and conduct.

What is the relevance of these observations to citizenship? It is this: the priority of citizenship is the bonding of individuals to the state; the priority of ethnicity is the bonding of individuals to their cultural group, often defined most intensely by language and/or religion. The nineteenth-century belief that citizens as nationals conflated the two identities has frequently been exposed as a figment.

Studies of the relationship between modern citizenship and multiculturalism have revealed three main categories of minorities whose interests must be embraced if the political health of the state and the reality of citizenship are to be preserved. First are those called the 'first peoples', the aboriginals. Second are the immigrants from other lands. Third are those peoples who form geographically coherent blocks rendering their countries effectively multi-national states. States which have had some success in accommodating the competing needs of citizenship and ethnicity in each of these categories have made arrangements to concede rights or privileges to the minorities in the constitution, in law or in policy without unduly straining the integrity of the state.

Canada provides a useful case study of this balancing process. The reason is that the country has been and still is composed of a mosaic of peoples who have won rights of separate identity to such a degree that in 1992 one commentator speculated that Canada might become the first post-modern democracy (see Pocock, 1995, p. 47), that is, a cluster of groups with their own identities and participative roles replacing a holistic citizenship.

Canada's first peoples are Amerindian nations such as the Crees and Hurons and the Arctic-dwelling Inuits. But these peoples have jealously maintained their languages and vigorously demanded rights to their own lands against 'Canadian' expropriation. The intensity of their self-identity may be discerned by reference to one example from each. In 1969 the government planned to give the hitherto denied status of full citizenship to the Amerindians, a proposal they treated with scorn because it failed to make amends for the long history of injustices they had endured. The second example concerns the Inuits, who succeeded in achieving a measure of autonomy by the creation of the new province of Nunavut carved out of the Northwest Territories in 1999.

To add to its ethnic complexity Canada has had a continuous history of immigration, initially from Europe, more recently from Asia. Some of these immigrants have been concerned to preserve elements of their original culture; for instance, the request by Sikh applicants for membership of the Royal Canadian Mounted Police to wear turbans instead of the traditional RCMP brimmed hat.

What, however, has figured most prominently in the Canadian experience of mixed population has been the character of Quebec, originally a French colony, New France, and acquired in the mid-eighteenth century by Britain through her victory in the Seven Years War. The *Québécois* (and other French Canadians, for example in Saskatchewan) have retained a deeply rooted French culture. Since the creation of the federation in 1867 Canada has effectively been a bilingual country, consolidated by the Official Languages Act of 1969, which provided for bilingual notices, signs and official communications.

This provision was a response to a radical, separatist mood in Quebec, stimulated by a speech by President de Gaulle at the Montreal International Exhibition when he uttered the inflammatory exclamation, '*Vive le Québec libre!*' The *Partie québécois* and the *Front de libération du Québec* were swiftly formed. The use of French in the province was promoted with determination, in 1974 being designated by the Quebec government as the official language.

Pan-Canadian national and citizen identity has never lacked considerable support both out of loyalty and expedience, the latter motive driven by fear of the consequences of the disintegration of the federation. Yet Canada remains a test-case for the validity and flexibility of the concept, status and ideal of citizenship-as-nationality; if by 'nationality' one means the definition of Sieyes as political identification with the state. But citizenship has become so much more complex in both theory and practice than this basic formula allows. One complication has been the spread of tiered modes of citizenship with the adoption by so many states of federal constitutions.

Federalism

'Layered' citizenship

Thus far we have been following the story of citizenship as a status held by an individual *vis-à-vis* a single, cohesive political or administrative unit – a city-state, a municipality, a nation state. However, in terms of constitutional structure some polities have devised two-tiered systems of government. In Europe the loose confederal arrangements of the Holy Roman Empire and Switzerland provided the obvious examplars until the late eighteenth century when the Americans tightened the control of the central government by moving to a federal form of constitution. Since then federalism has become an extremely popular form of state.

For convenience, we shall in this section refer to three different kinds of tiered constitutions, providing what we may term 'layered' citizenship, that is, the status of citizenship on both state and provincial strata – three levels, indeed, where a vigorous local, municipal and/or rural citizenship exists. These tiered constitutions are: federalism proper; the European Union as an arrangement *sui generis*; and the device called devolution. These systems enable power to be shared between the upper and lower levels, one objective of which is to combine centralized authority and decision-making with a retention of community identity for the component states or provinces. Citizenship then becomes complicated. Participation, identity and allegiance all have to accommodate both layers.

Since government exists at both levels, citizens have the opportunity to vote and be elected at both levels. Indeed, one of the major arguments in the twentieth century in favour of federalism and devolution has been precisely that it strengthens the democratic character of the state. On the other hand, a tiered structure presupposes that citizens are sufficiently keen to take an interest in both levels of public affairs simultaneously, and the ability of the constitution-in-operation clearly to demarcate what areas of activity properly belong to which layer. If that judgment fails to produce a balance acceptable to at least the bulk of the politically alert citizenry, the state may become unstable, even disintegrate, as nearly happened to the USA in the 1860s and did happen to Yugoslavia in the 1990s.

For federalism recognizes that the citizen will have a dual identity – both Virginian and American, Croatian and Yugoslav, for instance, in the above examples. The individual needs willingly and comfortably to accept this double civic identity and feel that both are justly recognized by the political system. It often happens that federal or devolved constitutions have been adopted because of clear cultural differences within the state. The extraordinary ethnic diversity of Nigeria has been a case in point, and is another example, a century after the American Civil War, of near break-up.

The maintenance of twin civic identities is not, then, only a matter of constitutional provisions and government policies; it is also a matter of the citizen giving effective allegiance to both layers: too hearty a sense of loyalty to the central state will weaken the emotional strength of the province or component state; the reverse will undermine the centripetal power of the state itself. In fact, the strength of local interest, especially when bolstered by ethnic cultural distinctiveness, has meant that, in the twentieth century, the latter condition has placed strains on the integrity of a number of states. This has led, for example, to the civil war in Nigeria, the fragmentation of Pakistan, the USSR and Yugoslavia, and schemes of devolution for several west European states including Spain, Belgium and the United Kingdom. This issue of the relationship between citizenship and national/ethnic/cultural identity and allegiance relates, of course, to the material in the first section of this chapter.

Two of the most significant examples of layered citizenship may be found in the history of the USA – a case of classic federalism, and the European Union – a much weaker style. These will be treated below. However, before leaving this introductory section, a few words are apposite about Switzerland, a fascinating example of how citizenship evolved in very particular ways.

That most distinguished nineteenth-century historian, Jakob Burckhardt, who was born in Basle, had this to say about Switzerland:

> The small State exists so that there may be one spot on earth where the largest possible proportion of the inhabitants are citizens in the fullest sense of the word. . . . The small State possesses nothing but real freedom, an ideal possession which fully balances the huge advantage of the big State.   (quoted, Bonjour, Offler and Potter, 1952, p. 338)

Citizenship at the local level had two medieval roots: the guilds in the towns, and in the rural communities the mass folk assemblies (the *Landsgemeinde*, with some affinities to the Athenian *polis* assembly). Citizenship at the state level was created with the adoption of a federal constitution in the nineteenth century, which, in turn, had its medieval roots in cantonal leagues and confederal linkages. The vital period for the modern development of both citizenship and federalism was the half-century 1798–1848.

In the eighteenth century Switzerland was a loose confederation of 13 cantons, comprising politically, oligarchically governed towns and quite democratic mountainous rural communities, though few people were interested in public affairs. For example, in the canton of Uri, the villagers elected a *Landammann* (chief magistrate) each year, yet only a limited number of families supplied candidates. But Switzerland could not be insulated from revolutionary ideas and from 1789 thoughts of the rights of man and the citizen were in the air. Then, in 1798, the French invaded, exported their revolution to the Swiss in the form of a unitary constitution – the Helvetic Republic – and a constitution with rights *à la française*.

After the Napoleonic Wars, the old system with some adaptations was restored, supported by conservatives but resented by liberals. Revolution in France in 1830 again stimulated hopes of more reform, a mood which in due course broke out in a brief war between the liberal Protestant cantons and the conservative Catholic cantons, the latter establishing their own union (*Sonderbund*). The liberal cantons prevailed, and from the experience a fully federal constitution was drafted in 1848, incorporating the status of citizen of the Swiss state.

Table 5.1. Citizen-participation in Switzerland

	Federal	Cantonal
Parliamentary System	Council of State – 2 representatives from each of 23 cantons	Canton Councils elected in 21 cantons
	National Councils – number of representatives proportional to size of cantons	*Landsgemeinde* (open air assembly) in 5 cantons
Referendum	Decisions on laws and international treaties submitted to popular vote if demanded by 50,000 voters or 8 cantons	Range of issues covered varies among the 21 cantons with Councils
Initiative	Constitutional amendments can be initiated if demanded by 100,000 voters	For constitutional affairs and legislation

The Constitution was put to the vote in the cantons and was adopted by the majority. The Zürich newspaper, *Neue Zürcher Zeitung*, summed up the atmosphere (albeit ignoring the continuing local form of citizenship):

The heart beats higher. Finally the Swiss nation has spoken and has received the right to vote which is its due. The nation, which so far has lived only in the hearts of its good citizens, now stands before us as an undeniable reality, with a decisive vote, with a broad authority. No longer will the Swiss citizens of different cantons appear as members of one nation only when they live or travel abroad; they will be Swiss and only Swiss also at home, especially in our relationships to foreign lands. Wherever we now go in Switzerland, we are at home, we are no longer aliens. (quoted, Kohn, 1956, pp. 109–10)

The 1848 Constitution, with periodic detailed amendments, remains the basis of the Swiss form of government today. Two features, reflecting the strength of citizenship, in addition to the *Landsgemeinde*, still in being, are virtually unique to Switzerland and give it the character of a direct democracy: these have been the referendum and the initiative. Present-day political rights of citizenship, inherited from the past, may be summarized as shown in *Table 5.1*.

United States

In the USA the precise relationship of the federal government and the citizen on the one hand and the state government and the citizen on the other has never really been resolved. Since 1777 Constitutional Articles, Supreme Court judgments and Presidential policies have striven to define and interpret this key issue of the federal system of government, yet disagreements still arise – evidence of the extreme difficulty of defining citizenship in a federal state.

When the War of Independence broke out in 1776 it was a conflict between the mother-country and thirteen separate colonies. Clearly, some coordination among the Americans was essential. Consequently, Articles of Confederation were drawn up, though not finally ratified until 1781, providing a tentative central government. The question of citizenship was covered by Article IV, dubbed the 'comity clause' because of its purpose of fostering a feeling of community among the several states. In part, this Article reads:

> The better to secure and perpetuate mutual friendship and intercourse among the people of different states in this union, the free inhabitants of each of these states (paupers, vagabonds and fugitives from justice excepted) shall be entitled to all privileges and immunities of free citizens in the several states. (quoted, Kettner, 1978, p. 220)

But this clarification only raised another problem. James Madison pounced on an ambiguity – the apparent and wrong implication that 'people' and 'inhabitants' were synonymous with 'citizens'.

> There is a confusion of language here which is remarkable [he declared, and continued]. . . . It seems to be a construction scarcely

> avoidable. . . that those who come under the denomination of free inhabitants of a State, although not citizens of such State, are entitled, in every other State, to all the privileges of free citizens of the latter; that is, to greater privileges than they may be entitled to in their own State. (*The Federalist*, no. 43)

Extraordinarily careless drafting, of course; and an early signal of the absolute need for lucidity and precision of thought in a federal state.

In any case, many Americans believed that the Articles of Confederation were too loose a structure. So, arrangements were set on foot to draft a Constitution for a tighter federal state. This process caused heated disagreements and criticisms; and to defend the framers of the document a series of essays was published in 1787–88, which together are called *The Federalist*. One of the authors was Madison, from one of whose contributions the above quotation is drawn.

Did the Constitution cope with the problem of two-layered citizenship any more effectively than the Articles of Confederation? It assuredly tidied up the comity clause quite briskly. Article IV.2 states: 'The citizens of each State shall be entitled to all privileges and immunities of citizens in the several States.' A pity, therefore, that the Constitution included a confusion of its own. The preamble opens with the famous declaration: 'We, the people of the United States. . . do ordain and establish this Constitution of the United States of America.' And yet, Article VII required the document to be ratified by Conventions assembled in the separate states.

Was the Constitution, then, brought into being by the whole nation ('the people of the United States') or by the plural peoples of the constituent states acting through their Conventions? Put bluntly: Was the Constitution, defining the USA politically, the creation of the citizens acting as a nation or people acting as groups of citizens of thirteen states? This was not just a nicety of constitutional law, but a question about which level could claim the fuller sovereignty, nation or state. A most bloody civil war was fought, at least partly, on this issue, a mere human life-span later.

For citizenship is not just a matter of constitutional law; it is also a matter of how citizens feel about their civic attachments. Two of the most eminent commentators on the young United States believed that the greater immediacy of the state government compared with the federal had the stronger pull on citizens' allegiance. The first of these writers was, again, Madison:

> Many considerations. . . seem to place it beyond doubt that the first and most natural attachment of the people will be to the government

of their respective States. Into the administration of these a greater number of individuals will expect to rise. . . . By the superintending care of these, all the more domestic and personal interests of the people will be regulated and provided for. With the affairs of these, the people will be more familiarly and minutely conversant. . . on the side of these, therefore, the popular bias may well be expected most strongly to incline.   (*The Federalist*, no. 46)

In 1831–32 the French scholar-politician Alexis de Tocqueville visited New England. The fruit of his studies was his *Democracy in America*, published in two volumes in 1835 and 1840. On the matter of primary attachment we find him of the same mind as Madison. He explained:

The central government of each state, being close to the governed, is continually informed of the needs that arise; every year new plans are put forward. . . and published in the press, exciting universal interest and eagerness among the citizens.   (quoted, Oldfield, 1990, p. 128)

No hint of injustice or danger can be read into either of these pronouncements. The unhappy potential implications were manifested only when the issue of slavery and black civil rights became entangled with the uncertainty of federal or state citizenship priority. The first clear signal that this deep division in American society was to have constitutional and citizenship repercussions was given in 1857. In that year the Chief Justice ruled in the Dred Scott case. The background and outcome, in extremely summary form, were as follows.

In 1820 an understanding called the Missouri Compromise prohibited slavery in the northern states. In 1834 Dred Scott, a slave, was taken by his master to the northern state of Illinois. Later, back in his home state of Missouri, Scott claimed his freedom by virtue of his residence in a free state. After lengthy and disputed judicial considerations, the Chief Justice gave his judgment. He asserted that Scott could not be a United States citizen because members of 'the African race' were excluded by the Constitution from such a status. Moreover, although any given state might concede rights to a black, no other state was bound to recognize that individual's new status. Specifically, he ruled that the Missouri Compromise was unconstitutional if it implied, as Scott claimed, a slave's enfranchisement by virtue of crossing the border into a free state; because a slave is property and property is safeguarded by the Fifth Amendment.

A decade later, as a result of the Civil War, these rulings were reversed. The right of states to deny citizenship was expunged; the denial of any right to citizenship of all blacks was rescinded, and the very institution of slavery was abolished.

The Fourteenth Amendment enacted in 1868, as we have seen, cleared away any dubiety. Not that, in practice, this prevented widespread discrimination and cruel persecution of blacks for another century. A Supreme Court judgment in 1896 set the tone:

> The object of the [Fourteenth] Amendment. . . could not have been intended to abolish distinctions based upon color. . . . Laws permitting, even requiring, [the] separation [of the two races]. . . have been generally. . . recognized as within the competency of the state legislatures in the exercise of their police power.   (quoted, Chandler, 1971, p. 132)

The struggle for black civil rights was not primarily a conflict between federal and state levels of citizenship. Nevertheless, one incident did famously test the Fourteenth Amendment.

The problem started in 1954, when the Supreme Court pronounced that 'separate educational facilities are inherently unequal'. Black and white pupils, in other words, should not be segregated in different schools. Three years later, plans for desegregation in Little Rock, Arkansas were bitterly opposed by some local citizens. Governor Faubus called out the National Guard to bar the entry to the Central High School of nine black pupils. Whose citizens' rights should prevail? The white protesters', backed by the state Governor, or the black children's, defined by the federal Supreme Court? The President, Eisenhower, could not allow this defiance of a Supreme Court ruling, nor the growing tumult in Little Rock. As he said, to have held his hand would have been 'tantamount to acquiescence in anarchy and the dissolution of the union' (quoted, Polenberg, 1980, p. 161). He dispatched federal troops to escort the black pupils into the school.

Even so, education, along with all other social services, had traditionally been accepted as being the responsibility of the states. The rights of social citizenship were accorded to the citizen at state, not federal level. If federal funds supplemented state monies for these services, they were channelled through state governments. However, in the 1960s the doctrine of 'Creative Federalism' undermined this traditional principle by the provision of grants-in-aid to support federal government social policy irrespective of the states' priorities. The Reagan administration of the 1980s attempted a reversal of this policy in its doctrine of 'New Federalism'. And so, the see-saw between state and federal citizenship has continued in motion.

Yet, in spite of all these problems experienced by the United States, its federal system attracted many European admirers. In fact, by the nineteenth century a movement was under way for the creation of a 'United States of Europe'.

European citizenship

A union of European states does not necessarily involve the creation of a legal category of European citizen. From the seventeenth to the twentieth century political thinkers and statesmen produced a steady stream of plans for collaborative institutions, though not until the foundation of the Council of Europe in 1949, the European Coal and Steel Community (ECSC) in 1952 and the European Economic Community (EEC) in 1957 was any scheme put into effect. But none of their founding documents made reference to European citizenship. Not until 1961 did the concept appear in European Community (EC) documents.

Be that as it may, a thin form of European citizenship was already evolving through the Council of Europe and the EC. We may indeed conveniently think of European citizenship as having developed in four forms. These are: the establishment of European human rights by the Council of Europe; the formation of a European Parliament by the EC; the practices of the EC/EU; and the instituting of formal citizenship of the European Union (EU) by the Maastricht Treaty in 1993. A few words, then, about the justification for using the word 'citizenship' in the first three contexts.

During the half-century since the creation of the Council of Europe the number of member-states has steadily increased from the original ten to 45 in 2003. All inhabitants of these countries are consequently, legally at least, covered by the 1950 European Convention for the Protection of Human Rights, abuses of which can be tried, via the Commission of Human Rights, in the European Court of Human Rights, set up in 1959. These measures may be considered to promote the civil rights of European citizens, especially by virtue of Article 25 of the Convention:

> The Commission may receive petitions. . . from any person, non-governmental organisation or group of individuals claiming to be the victim of a violation by one of the High Contracting Parties of the rights set forth in this Convention, provided that the High Contracting Party against which the complaint has been lodged has declared that it recognises the competence of the Commission to receive such petitions.

In other words, you are only fully a European citizen in this context if your own state permits you to be. For example, the UK did not concede this until 1966.

A common and important feature of political citizenship is the right to vote for parliamentary representatives. At first, members of the European Assembly (of the EC) were MPs from their own national parliaments. Nevertheless, even in the Treaty of Paris, which created the first Community body, the ECSC, provision was made for direct elections. The first were held in 1979, though, it must be said, that the turn-out in some member states, notably the UK, has not shown much Euro-civic commitment.

Since the EC started in the post-war years as an essentially economic enterprise, it is not surprising that individuals have been perceived more as workers than citizens. The European Commission has issued Directives, the European Court of Justice has built up a body of case law and the Maastricht Treaty has the appendage of the Social Chapter. Together they compose a formidable set of rights, which may be construed as social and economic rights of citizens, just as much as of workers, of the European Union.

The Maastricht Treaty came into effect in 1993. It furthered the process of integration, enshrined in its inauguration of the European Union covering a wide range of actual or planned collaboration. The treaty also formally established the status of citizenship of the Union.

The decision to take this step arose from concerns within the EC institutions about the lack of popular commitment to the Community, the remote technocratic style of the Commission's work and the so-called 'democratic deficit'. This third factor refers to the weakness of the European Parliament and other forms of accountability to which the Council of Ministers and the Commission feel obliged to respond. In 1984 the European Council (the heads of government of the member states), at their meeting in Fontainebleau, resolved to promote measures for the fostering of a 'People's Europe', the term in its French version being, tellingly, 'Europe des Citoyens'. Sundry innovations followed, such as the issuing of EC passports.

However, it was Article 8 of the Maastricht Treaty that defined the political rights which were henceforth to be available to citizens of the European Union. *Table 5.2* incorporates the main words of the text.

Even so, by the turn of the century the reality of European citizenship both in practice and in sentiment was the palest of shadows beside national citizenship, scarcely more sharply in evidence than world citizenship.

Table 5.2. Citizenship of the European Union

Article	General Rights	Article	Electoral Rights
8a1	Every citizen of the Union shall have the right to move and reside freely within the territory of the Member States.	8b1	Every citizen of the Union residing in a Member State of which he is not a national shall have the right to vote and to stand as a candidate at municipal elections in the Member State in which he resides.
8c	Every citizen of the Union shall, in the territory of a third country in which the Member State of which he is a national is not represented, be entitled to the protection of the diplomatic or consular authorities of any Member State.	8b2	. . . every citizen of the Union residing in the Member State of which he is not a national shall have the right to vote and to stand as a candidate in elections to the European Parliament in the Member State in which he resides.
8d	Every citizen of the Union shall have the right to petition the Parliament . . . Every citizen of the Union may apply to the Ombudsman.		

World citizenship

Classical revivals

We owe it to the Stoics (see Chapter Two) for developing the concept of world citizenship, albeit as little more than a figure of speech and certainly not a legal or political status. Their vision did not embrace constituting a world state in any formalized sense. Insofar as that dream did exist during the first one-and-a-half millennia AD, it took the form of the ambition for a universal Roman or renewed Roman Empire, in which the issue of citizenship was not considered.

From the late fifteenth to the mid-sixteenth century the Renaissance revival of classical culture witnessed the printing and translation of many Greek and Latin texts, among them the works of Stoic writers. One of the last of this wave was Marcus Aurelius' *Meditations*, published in 1558.

The Stoic writers were eagerly absorbed by sixteenth- and seventeenth-century philosophers and writers, referred to, naturally, as 'Neostoics'.

The most influential of the Neostoics was Justus Lipsius, who lived the greater part of his life in the Low Countries. 'The whole world is our country,' he declared (Lipsius, 1939, I. ix). He also repeated the story which was perhaps first retailed by Epictetus in the first century AD that Socrates, when asked to what country he belonged, responded that he never said he was an Athenian, but, 'I am a citizen of the universe'. The French essayist Montaigne, in turn, influenced by the work of Lipsius, cited the Socrates anecdote in support of his own cosmopolitan predilections.

However, it was in the second wave of classical revival, the Enlightenment, that the notion of world citizenship became widely broadcast. For a century, expressed with different emphases, the cosmopolitan ideal caught the imagination of numerous thinkers, including the giants of political thought, Locke and Kant, at each end of the hundred-year span. Writing of the law of nature, Locke asserted:

> by which law, common to them all, [a man] and all the rest of mankind are one community, make up one society distinct from all other creatures and were it not for the corruption and viciousness of degenerate men, there would be no need of any other, no necessity that man should separate from this great and natural community, and associate into lesser combinations. (Locke, 1962, paragraph 128)

He does not use the term 'world citizenship', yet the argument has a clearer meaning of political world citizenship than in the comments of the men of the eighteenth-century Enlightenment explicitly using the words. The likes of Voltaire, Franklin and Schiller declared themselves citizens of the world mainly in the sense of enjoying transnational contacts and a transnational culture. Thomas Paine, it is true, used the idea with political overtones. This was partly because he participated in the political affairs of America and France as well as his native England, and partly because of his interpretation of the American Revolution as the inauguration of a new era, when its ideals, having spread throughout the globe, would inspire the evolution of a world citizenship.

Many of the French Revolutionaries also felt that their revolution was performing a similar role. For instance, Robespierre, sought, admittedly unsuccessfully, to add to the 1793 Jacobin Declaration of Rights the following article:

> Men of all countries are brothers, and the different peoples must help one another according to their ability, as though they were citizens of one and the same State. (Bouloiseau *et al.*, 1952, p. 469)

Since Robespierre was extremely well grounded in the classics it is tempting to think that he had in mind the comment by the Stoic Plutarch, who wrote that 'we should consider all men to be one community and one polity' (Plutarch, 1957, 329(6)).

The production of a fully-fledged plan for a universal state peopled by world citizens was left to the eccentric imagination of Anacharchis Cloots, the self-styled 'Orator of Mankind', in his *Constitutional Foundations for the Republic of the Human Race*. Once fully formed by popular demand, this world republic would ensure global peace:

> Calculate beforehand the happiness which citizens will enjoy, when the avarice of trade and the jealousies of neighbourhood are restrained by universal law, when ambitions are eclipsed by the majority of the human race.   (Cloots, 1793, p. 15)

Cloots produced his scheme in 1793, though failed to raise any enthusiasm in its support from the Convention to whom he presented the document.

Two years later an incomparably more sober and profoundly thought-through scheme was published by Kant. The Prussian philosopher's notion of world citizenship is incorporated in his *Perpetual Peace: A Philosophical Sketch*. Here he identifies three kinds of law, the third of which is cosmopolitan law (or right, the German word *Recht*). His brief definition of this as incorporated in a constitution, is:

> a constitution based on cosmopolitan right, in so far as individuals and states, coexisting in an external relationship of mutual influences, may be regarded as citizens of a universal state of mankind (*ius cosmopoliticum*).   (Reiss, 1991, pp. 98–9n.)

Kant had two main principles in mind in positing a cosmopolitan law. One was that, because of the increase in mobility, all human beings have a right of hospitality in whatever country they find themselves. And, secondly, that, because there has come to exist a quasi-universal community, 'a violation of rights in one part of the world is felt everywhere' (Reiss, 1991, p. 108). One implication of this second principle is the duty of the world citizen to be vigilant in identifying the abuse of rights anywhere in the world. It is little wonder that Kant's ideas reverberate in the world two centuries after he formulated them.

Response to total war

Yet the boost to the concept of world citizenship afforded by the Enlightenment was of feeble strength in comparison with the ideological power of nationalism, which virtually obliterated the cosmopolitan ideal for one-and-a-half, if not two, centuries. The evil inherent in nationalism was made starkly manifest by the two World Wars. The horrified reactions to each of these conflicts created a climate of opinion conducive to the actual foundation of international bodies. But neither the League of Nations nor the United Nations Organization found room in their principles or institutions for the enfranchisement of humankind as citizens of the world.

Those who hoped in 1918 and in 1945 for at least some elected world assembly were disappointed. And this disappointment led to thoughts and proposals for a revised world body which would incorporate just such a representative element and thus bring into being a world citizenry in the sense of a world electorate. The authors of these schemes – and we shall see later that the proposal is still very much alive – have varied in their expectations of implementation from the naïvely optimistic to the realistically cautious. One of the most widely read of the numerous American projects for a world federal or quasi-federal government was Mortimer J. Adler's *How to Think about War and Peace*, published in 1944. In this work he made the cool assessment that, 'It seems reasonable to predict that the members of the human race can be made ready for world citizenship within five hundred years' (quoted, Laursen, 1970, p. 82)!

From 1945 the need for cosmopolitan thinking and action took on an even greater appearance of urgency because of the frigidity of the Cold War confrontation and the prospect of nuclear holocaust. The connection between this hideously perilous situation and the notion of world citizenship was simply voiced by Bernard Baruch. In 1946 US President Truman appointed him to the UN commission for international control of atomic materials. He addressed this body in the following words: 'My Fellow Members of the United Nations Atomic Energy Commission, and My Fellow Citizens of the World: We are here to make the choice between the quick and the dead' (quoted, Walker, 1993, p. 165).

In the immediate post-War years three, often interconnected, movements got under way which were directly or indirectly bound to the concept of world citizenship. One was the attempt to persuade individuals to declare themselves to be world citizens and to mobilize them as a force to promote global interests. The second was the production of schemes for a federal world government. The third was an expression of discontent with the UN and the drafting of plans for its reform.

In 1945 the Frenchman Robert Sarrazac founded the *Front Humain des Citoyens du Monde*, which included in its agenda the idea that individuals should register themselves as world citizens. An American, Garry Davis, put this scheme into practice by starting the World Citizens' Registry, collecting 800,000 adherents within months. The Registry still exists. However, Davis was by no means content with the bureaucratic work of issuing world citizens' identity cards. With deliberate publicity-seeking theatricality, he renounced his US citizenship, pitched his tent at the entrance of the Palais de Chaillot (the venue of the UN General Assembly at that time (1948)), demanding that the world body recognize him as a world citizen. This was news. His photograph and story appeared prominently in the world's newspapers.

Davis' objective was the creation of a world federal government. He retrospectively explained: 'I would bring about world government, I reasoned, precisely as all other governments had been brought into being: simply by declaring myself an actual citizen of that government and behaving like one' (Davis, 1961, p. 19). Historically misleading, but he was not alone in asserting the connection. The goal of a world government with an elected parliament can be traced back to the late eighteenth century. It persisted through the nineteenth and early twentieth centuries. For example, in 1842 Alfred, Lord Tennyson wrote in his 'Locksley Hall' of his vision of 'the Parliament of Man, the Federation of the World'.

In the more democratic and urgent age following the Second World War, the agenda was developed to enhance the role of at least a portion of the putative world electorate by their involvement in the task of drawing up the constitution for the federation of the world. This proposal featured, for example, in the Montreux Declaration. In 1948 a meeting took place in this little Swiss town with the purpose of founding the World Movement for World Federal Government (now known as the World Federalist Movement). Its founding document listed two lines of action. One reads as follows:

> the preparation of a world constituent assembly, the plan of campaign for which shall be laid down by the Council of the Movement in close cooperation with the parliamentary groups and federalist movements in the different countries. . . . This plan [i.e. the draft constitution] shall be submitted for ratification, not only to the governments and parliaments, but also the peoples themselves.

The declaration reinforced the message of popular participation by asserting: 'One thing is certain, we shall never realise world federal government unless the peoples of the world join in the crusade' (quoted, Walker, 1993, p. 175).

But 'we the peoples of the world' were already, according to the preamble of the UN Charter, the very foundation of that established organization. Only, the trouble has been that its institutional structure gives the peoples of the world precious little say. Self-proclaimed world citizens have consequently been severely critical of the only world political organization that has existed since 1945. In the face of the impracticability of building a more democratic parallel body, most world federalists have pinned their hopes on a radical reform of the UN and its procedure. This has been integral to the programme of the World Federalist Movement since its inception. The most realistic element of these demands has been the creation of a world citizens' assembly, to exist side-by-side with the General Assembly of representatives of the world's states. It was a proposal that regained prominence at the end of the twentieth century.

The end of the twentieth century

Two developments reinvigorated the idea of world citizenship during the last quarter-century of the second millennium. First came the accelerating consciousness of global environmental problems, a sheaf of observed and calculated hazards, some of which are as terrifying in the long term as the thermo-nuclear threat seemed to be in the short term in the most tense years of the Cold War. The second development was the collapse of the Communist Cold War antagonist in 'counter-revolutions' of 1989–91 and the exciting expectation of a more collaborative international regime.

We must, however, place these developments in context. Interest in believing oneself a world citizen faded after the initial post-1945 enthusiasm, the Americans and the French being notable for retaining a certain commitment. It was in the US and France, in fact, that adherents to world citizenship revived their activity in the mid-1970s. At that time there was founded Planetary Citizens and *Le Mouvement populaire des Citoyens du Monde*. In 1975 the first meeting of the World Citizens' Assembly was held in San Francisco.

Participants in these developments, inevitably, tended to be supporters of the World Federalist Movement. However, belief in the possibility, even desirability, of a global state, though commanding some attention, was rapidly waning. World federalists had come, by the last quarter of the twentieth century, to focus on the reform of the UN and the development of an effective world law.

The World Citizens' Assembly was instrumental in putting new heart into the campaign for a UN Citizens' (or Peoples' or Second) Assembly. By collaborative efforts there followed the creation of the International Network for a UN Assembly (INFUSA) in 1982 and the Campaign for a More Democratic United Nations (CAMDUN) in 1989. INFUSA's policy has attracted considerable interest among Non-Governmental Organizations (NGOs) as it seems more feasible than most other projects with similar objectives. INFUSA proposes the election by the world's peoples of a merely consultative body, as a subsidiary to the General Assembly, and as provided for by Article 22 of the UN Charter. In contrast, CAMDUN's aim is to effect a revision of the Charter in order to change its representative element to a bicameral system: to form an elected assembly working alongside the body of states' delegates, the General Assembly.

One of the persistent criticisms of the UN, in addition to its undemocratic nature, is its relative ineffectualness in promoting an expectation of world citizens' rights and duties. This is the result of the built-in principle of state sovereignty and the institution's domination by the great powers. For instance, just as the eighteenth-century American and French Constitutions were accompanied by a list of rights, so the UN Charter is accompanied by the Universal Declaration of Human Rights. Therefore, in the same way as citizens of a state expect their rights to be upheld by the state, so citizens of the world should be able to expect their rights to be upheld by the UN. Yet the abuse of human rights, in violation of the Declaration – from arbitrary arrest to genocide – has been endemic.

Moreover, apart from the Nuremberg Principles, which guided the prosecution of war criminals after the Second World War, no detailed code of World Law has existed. However, to punish such abuses a permanent World Court to mete out criminal justice was provided for by the Rome Statute of 1998 when 110 countries agreed to create an International Criminal Court (ICC). This event was an implicit recognition that we are all world citizens in the sense of being bound by an embryonic world law and answerable for any transgressions. The Court came into existence in 2003 despite the hostility of a number of countries, most notably the United States.

The concept of world citizenship has enjoyed only a halting history. It has been vaguely and variously interpreted to mean anything from a willingness to commit oneself to a universal moral code to a conviction that the building of a world state is essential. Moreover, not until the

1990s was any really concentrated thought devoted to the matter. By questioning the likely future implications for democratic institutions, control and behaviour of the rapidly progressing processes of cultural, economic and communications globalization, a small number of scholars, notably the British academic, David Held, have generated the concept of 'cosmopolitan democracy'. And, of course, if cosmopolitan democracy is to flourish, it needs cosmopolitan citizens.

The key work expounding the concept of cosmopolitan democracy is Held's *Democracy and the Global Order*. He envisages democratic principles infusing the world's political and legal systems. Thus, if all states came to adopt democratic procedures and accepted the validity of a global, democratically approved law, then 'the rights and responsibilities of people *qua* national citizens and *qua* subjects of cosmopolitan law could coincide, and democratic citizenship could take on, in principle, a truly universal status' (Held, 1995, p. 233). The working-out of the detail of cosmopolitan democracy is intricate. Only a thin indication of the conceptual map is possible here, and only as it illuminates the notion of world citizenship.

We must imagine the system two-dimensionally. In one dimension – the range of activities – cosmopolitan citizens must be given opportunities to participate politically, ensure a just legal system and hold the workings of the economy to account. In the other dimension – the geographical and institutional scope – they must be given opportunities to operate at local, regional, national and global levels and also, crucially, in the civil society arena of non-governmental and functional organizations such as trade unions, professional bodies and pressure groups. Democracy would reinforce democracy in this complex network. Citizenship would be enriched; and world citizenship would be given a living reality well beyond the mental and moral constructs of the Stoics, though, by no means, one hopes, in ignorance of or ignoring their ethical standards as an ideal.

CHAPTER SIX

Modern and Contemporary Themes II

Civil, political and social rights

Marshall's analysis

Two hundred years elapsed after the publication of Rousseau's *Social Contract* before the next statement on citizenship of any considerable influence appeared. In 1949 T.H. Marshall, Professor of Sociology at the London School of Economics and Political Science, delivered a series of lectures at Cambridge, an expanded version of which was published the following year under the title, *Citizenship and Social Class*. Marshall conveyed two important messages. One was his thesis that the equality inherent in citizenship can be compatible with the inequality inherent in class structure. The other was his perception that the rights of citizenship are composed of three 'bundles' and evolved historically in order: civil, political and social. His whole analysis, it must be emphasized, was based on English history. (Marshall had been an historian before transferring his academic interests to Sociology.)

Excerpts illustrating the first of these theses reveal his train of thought:

> there is a kind of basic human equality associated with the concept of full membership of a community – or, as I should say, of citizenship – which is not inconsistent with the inequalities which distinguish the various economic levels in the society. In other words, the inequality of the social class system may be acceptable provided the equality of citizenship is recognised.   (Marshall and Bottomore, 1992, p. 6)

More than that, he argued, the co-existence of inequalities of class and the equality of citizenship had become so firmly accepted that 'citizenship has itself become, in certain respects, the architect of legitimate social inequality' (Marshall and Bottomore, 1992, p. 7).

Marshall defined his second thesis, the tripartite interpretation of citizenship, as follows:

> The civil element is composed of the rights necessary for individual freedom – liberty of the person, freedom of speech, thought and faith, the right to own property and to conclude valid contracts, and the right to justice. . . . By the political element I mean the right to participate in the exercise of political power, as a member of a body invested with political authority or as an elector of the members of such a body. . . . By the social element I mean the whole range from the right to share to the full in the social heritage and to live the life of a civilised being according to the standards prevailing in the society.   (Marshall and Bottomore, 1992, p. 8)

How, then, did Marshall view these three elements evolving in stages in England? Very broadly, he saw civil rights developing in the eighteenth century, political rights in the nineteenth, and social rights in the twentieth century. However, he recognizes that some 'elasticity' must be allowed in defining these stages. For example, late seventeenth-century legislation like the *Habeas Corpus* and Toleration Acts and Catholic Emancipation and the Repeal of the Combination Acts (i.e. legalization of trade unions) in the early nineteenth century are part of the 'eighteenth-century' phase.

The chronology of social citizenship, he concedes, is even more elastic. He even suggests that the Speenhamland system of poor relief, introduced in 1795, incorporated 'a substantial body of social rights' (Marshall and Bottomore, 1992, p. 14). He also judges the nineteenth-century state intervention to protect workers by means of the Factory Acts and to provide children with an elementary level of education as notable extensions of social rights. Nevertheless, the legislation of 1944–46 most impressed Marshall and was the background against which he shaped his whole analysis. The Beveridge Report of 1942 led directly to the Welfare State reforms and the Butler Act in 1944 introduced 'secondary education for all'.

In such a compressed précis, it has been impossible to do justice to the richness and subtlety of Marshall's work. We must not, however, leave him without noting two crucial observations he made about his triad of citizens' rights.

One is that social rights are different in kind from civil and political rights. Civil and political rights can be defined and recognized with some precision. The right to trial by jury or the right to vote, for example, either do or do not exist in law and in practice. In contrast, social rights relate to the quality of life. Access to education and a health service, for example, are social rights, but exactly what standards should be expected of schools and hospitals cannot be prescribed by reference to the principle of social citizenship.

The other observation is that social rights, previously virtually ignored as a component of citizenship, are in fact essential for the effective enjoyment of civil and political rights, because poverty and ignorance inevitably impair the will and opportunity to benefit from them.

Marshall's insights were invaluable. One British academic, writing nearly half-a-century after the lectures, declared that 'the most significant contribution to social and political theory made this century by a British sociologist is "citizenship" and. . . it was made by. . . T.H. Marshall' (quoted, Bulmer and Rees, 1996, jacket).

Even so, the confines of Marshall's study, in restricting himself to the English scene, must not be forgotten. We must go on to ask what his notion of a three-fold citizenship tells us about the history of citizenship in some other countries in modern and contemporary times.

Denial of rights

Citizenship is a legal status, synonymous with nationality in the modern nation-state. In general terms, residents in a country are either citizens or aliens. Hypothetically, therefore, an individual could be a citizen in a state where the government denies its citizens any of the three kinds of rights which liberal theory since Marshall has accepted are the components of the citizenly status. In such a circumstance citizenship would be a juridico-political title and identity void of its proper meaning. This is not, in fact, merely an abstract hypothesis: it has been a common condition in the twentieth century.

Autocratic regimes have sustained themselves in power by depriving their so-called citizens of civil and political rights especially, while in the cases of regimes constructed on the ideologies of racism and Communism, citizenship was further undermined by being a form of identity secondary to race and class respectively. Insofar as autocratic governments have called upon their populations to act as citizens, the objective has been to summon them to perform their civic duty of supporting the regime. The spectacular Nazi rallies, for instance, outdid anything in Rousseau's imagination for arousing and mobilizing civic enthusiasm. And as for voting rights, persistent reports of turn-outs and support for the Communist candidates of well over 90 per cent in Stalinist states after the Second World War give the lie to any claim to real political citizenship in those countries.

To return to our initial proposition: there is often more than a degree of hypocrisy in autocratic regimes between the range of rights as legally and constitutionally pronounced and their actual denial. The history of the Soviet Union provides an instructive illustration. At the time of the Revolution, following the precedent set by France, all titles were abolished, even that of 'Mr', and were replaced by 'citizen' (*grazhdenin*). However, by the time of the 1924 Constitution Lenin had replaced the civic with class terms: the people of the USSR were described instead as 'proletarians', 'peasants' or 'soldiers'.

Twelve years later, Stalin's 1936 Constitution boasted its democratic quality and the term 'citizen' was reinstated. The Constitution provided a comprehensive list of civil rights: equality before the law, freedom of conscience, of speech, of assembly and of the press, for example.

On political rights, the History of the CPSU reports with pride that:

> all citizens of the U.S.S.R. who have reached the age of eighteen, irrespective of race or nationality, religion, standard of education, domicile, social origin, property status or past activities, have the right to vote in the election of deputies and to be elected, with the exception of the insane and persons convicted by court of law to sentences including deprivation of electoral rights.   (Commission of the C.C. of the C.P.S.U.(B.), 1951, p. 526)

Social rights embraced the right to work, to leisure, to education and to maintenance in old age, during sickness or because of physical disability. Duties of citizenship, too, were listed: observing the laws, discipline at work, defending the fatherland, as well as the typically Communist obligation of 'respecting the rules of the Socialist community, [and] safeguarding and strengthening public, Socialist property' (Commission of the C.C. of the C.P.S.U.(B.), 1951, p. 527).

Yet these were the constitutional provisions under which the generality of the population lived in a state of apprehension, terror indeed. The NKVD and KGB exiled millions to languish and die in labour camps, dissidents were found guilty by a criminal code at variance with the proclaimed civil rights, and elections were confined to official candidates. True, there was some compensation in the effective provision of the social rights to education and health services. But citizenship in the basic civil and political senses was a façade.

Much the same can be said for other authoritarian governments, often military regimes, that have been so common in Latin America and many post-colonial states in Africa and Asia. The usual measure of the degree to which rights were abused throughout the world in the second half of the twentieth century has been the ways that states have fallen short of the requirements set forth in the Universal Declaration of Human Rights promulgated in 1948.

Now, although this document was drafted in order to proclaim the importance and range of *human* rights, the distinction between human and citizenship rights is insufficiently wide to prevent our using the Declaration as a yardstick here. Take fundamental civil rights. In the 1980s some 70 states were holding people in jail for an inordinate time before being brought to trial. In 1998, half-a-century after the Declaration, Amnesty International reminded the world that,

> Last year we recorded extra-judicial executions in 55 countries, judicial executions in 40, and 'disappearances' in 32 countries. We believe the true statistics to be much higher. (quoted, *Guardian*, 1998)

Citizenship rights and democracy

The countries of the North Atlantic region – the USA and western Europe, together with Britain's two antipodean Dominions – led the way in introducing and consolidating the rights of citizenship from the eighteenth to the twentieth century. When India became independent in 1947, it also made the brave decision, for such a large, diverse, ill-educated and poor country, to adopt a liberal democratic style of government.

Then, towards the end of the twentieth century, former Communist states of the Soviet Union and central/eastern Europe established new, democratic institutions, and some military dictatorships, notably in Latin America, were superseded. One assessment has suggested that the number of liberal democratic states rose in the half-century 1940–90 from 13 to 61 (see Fukuyama, 1992, pp. 50, 348 n.12). Figures like these must, however, be treated with some caution because no state has a perfect record of honouring all citizens' rights completely, so the criteria can be neither exactly tested nor the results of such judgments be beyond dispute. None the less, the general trend is evident: absence of civic rights or their existence in severely diminished form is widely decried, people are increasingly demanding their rights, and states are gradually conceding them.

One of the problems relating to citizenship and its associated rights is the difficulty of firmly embedding them in the socio-political culture of a state in a short span of time. Even countries with a long-lived liberal tradition, among which we may number the USA, France, Britain, Switzerland and the Low Countries, have taken many generations to reach their current levels of civic life; and these levels still fall short of the ideal, especially in the difficult field of social rights. Belief in the value of citizenship and willingness to make it a reality also take time to develop and may well be subject to periodic relapses.

Two comments from the USA, where citizenship has had more than two centuries to mature, are interesting indicators of this problem. One relates to government attitude towards social rights, the other, to citizens' attitudes towards political rights. In 1999 the English politician Roy Hattersley, reported that,

> Twenty-five years ago Ronald Reagan told me that, in a sophisticated economy, anyone who persistently looked for work would find it and that people who did not search with sufficient diligence sacrificed the rights of citizenship. (Hattersley, 1999, p. 15)

The comment on political citizenship is a report of an observation by an American political scientist originally published in 1988:

> [He] noted that over one five-year period a resident of Cambridge, England, could have voted 4 times as compared to the 165 times that a resident of Tallahassee, Florida, could have voted. . . . The overwhelming nature of this task is often given as a major explanation for the low voter turnouts in the United States compared with the other Western democracies. (Hahn, 1998, pp. 264–5)

If the USA has not yet moulded a just, effective and balanced form of citizens' rights, how much more difficult must it be for states and societies emerging from long periods of authoritarian government, during which the experience and practice of civic rights were severely curtailed. Let us take as examples the emergence of Hungary from four decades of Communist government in 1990 (and a weak culture of democracy prior to 1949) and Argentina's return to constitutional government in 1983 after well over half-a-century of civilian and military autocratic governments.

A prime feature of the People's Democracies of eastern Europe was their building effective forms of social citizenship in accordance with their socialist doctrine and ideals. Civil and political rights, in contrast, were limited, a limitation often brutally maintained by the Stalinist-style secret police. In the case of Hungary, the repressive policy of the widely hated Mátyás Rákosi was so offensive that popular opposition burst forth in the ill-fated uprising of 1956.

When the Communist edifice collapsed, a market economy replaced the socialist system and liberal civil and political rights were conferred on the citizenry: the turn-about was dramatic. In the words of one Hungarian academic:

> The Hungarian population gained much in terms of civil, political and human rights but suffered great losses concerning social rights. Many social services, previously free of charge for everybody and perceived as part of citizenship rights no longer exist.   (Mátrai, 1998, p. 53)

However, the new opportunity to participate in civic affairs has only slowly been taken up. To quote Ms Mátrai again:

> active participation has not characterized Hungarian political culture. During the pre-war era, politics was the prerogative and the exclusive domain of the élite, and at the present stage of Hungarian democracy, civil society is just beginning to emerge.   (Mátras, 1998, pp. 66–7)

To turn now to Argentina, chosen as an example of the way a number of Latin American countries (Bolivia, Brazil, Ecuador, Peru and Uruguay also) shrugged off military dictatorships and returned to civilian rule in the 1980s. In Argentina the restoration of democratic institutions in 1983 and the election of the civilian Carlos Menem as President in 1989 marked this significant transition.

The problems stemming from the absence of a democratic tradition, noted in the case of Hungary, however, have also been a powerful rein on the development of participative citizenship in Argentina, as this formidable catalogue of constraints indicates:

> Tolerance for difference, pragmatism and willingness to engage in debate and compromise, a sense of efficient political institutions, a general climate of cooperation, and bargaining and accommodation between competing parties – all of which characterize most democratic political cultures. . . – are to a large extent foreign to Argentina.   (Chaffee, Morduchowicz and Galperin, 1998, p. 151)

Add to this blank backcloth serious economic problems for the new democracy, and the outcome is widespread apathy. In 1997 one poll showed that 51 per cent of the population would not bother to vote if it were not obligatory.

One term in the second quotation from Mátrai's essay provides a clue to the difficulties experienced in creating an active exercise of citizens' political rights: that term is 'civil society'. Liberal political theorists such as Tocqueville and Mill understood that participative citizenship is unlikely fully to evolve at the state level without experience of similar activity at the more immediately relevant and intimate levels of village, parish, ward, factory or trade union. Citizenship has to be built from the bottom up. Moreover, a family atmosphere, provided by the female half of the population, and the ethos of schools and the teaching in them also have vital contributions to make in laying these foundations.

Women

Centuries of civic repression

Citizenship has existed for nearly three millennia; with very minor exceptions, women have had some share in civic rights in the most liberal states for only about a century. This juxtaposed contrast has sometimes been explained by the argument that citizenship, particularly in its civic republican mode, is a status invented by men for men. Aristotelean *aretē*, Ciceronic *virtus* and Machiavellian *virtù* are at one and the same time quintessentially male and citizenly qualities. The supposed polarization of male and female natures was tartly summarized by the English writer, Rebecca West. She reflected

> that the word 'idiot' comes from a Greek root meaning private person. Idiocy is the female defect: intent on their private lives, women follow their fate through a darkness deep as that cast by malformed cells in the brain. It is no worse than the male defect, which is lunacy: they are so obsessed by public affairs that they see the world as by moonlight, which shows the outline of every object but not the details indicative of their nature. (West, 1963, p. 3)

This assumed dichotomy between private females and public males was by custom buttressed by another distinction. Citizenship was traditionally based on property ownership and property was overwhelmingly in male hands. Even in liberal states with a common law tradition, down to the nineteenth century married women were rendered civically non-persons by the device of 'coverture': they were subsumed into the legal identity of their husbands, who 'covered' them – and owned their property.

A vivid example of this condition can be drawn from Canada. In 1916 a woman was appointed as a magistrate in the province of Alberta. When she appeared in court her right to her judicial status was challenged on the grounds that, as a woman, in the eyes of English common law, she was not a 'person'. Only 13 years later did the Privy Council concede that Canadian women could be 'persons' in law.

We are here primarily interested in how women have achieved a more equal civic standing during the past century or so. Nevertheless, we need first of all to sketch in the earlier historical background, in reaction to which this progress has been made.

In classical times women had no rights. Their place was in the home and their function to rear children. Engagement in public discussion and the critical appraisal of personalities, so essential for both the *polis* and the republican style of citizenship, were thought to be contradictions of the ideal of seemly womanhood. Pericles, at the conclusion of his Funeral Oration, addresses the women in the assembled mourners thus: 'the greatest glory of a woman is to be least talked about by men, whether they are praising you or criticizing you' (Thucydides, 1954, p. 122). Sophocles expressed the thought from the opposite angle when he wrote, 'A modest silence is a woman's crown' (quoted, Aristotle, 1948, 1260a11).

But the ancient objection to women being citizens on a par with men went deeper than that. Citizenship was not only designed in the image of men, the adult male citizen was the ideal human being – an interpretation embedded in Aristotle's definition of citizenship. Women, it was widely held, had neither the physical nor mental qualities to participate in that role; therefore, not only could they not be citizens because their nature precluded it, they were also by the same token the inferior half of the human race. Greek women would not, generally speaking, have had the muscular strength to serve as hoplites, for example, a duty expected of citizens. But deficient in mental qualities? Aristotle asserted this misogynistic assumption with unequivocal bluntness: 'The slave is entirely without the faculty of deliberation,' he proclaims; 'the female indeed possesses it, but in a form which remains inconclusive; and if children possess it, it is only in immature form' (Aristotle, 1948, 1260a).

Plato, on the other hand, held a view which ran against the grain of his times. In the *Republic*, during the discussion about the elite Ruler class, he goes out of his way to allow for the participation of women even at that level. The exchange is as follows:

That is a fine portrait of our Rulers, Socrates.

Yes, Glaucon, and you must not forget that some of them will be women. All I have been saying applies just as much to any women

who are found to have the necessary gifts. Quite right, if they are to
share equally with the men in everything, as we said. (Plato, 1941,
VII. 540)

They had, indeed, agreed that women in this ideal state should share the
same education and training.

So, we must not imagine a completely blanket exclusion of women
from any thought of citizenly activity. A similar picture of general,
though not universal, exclusion is to be found in medieval Europe,
though in this age the evidence lies in the practice rather than the theory
of citizenship.

Medieval women suffered from the Christian context in which
they perforce lived. St Paul transmitted the Greek prejudice with the
injunction of silence: 'Woman's voice is not to be heard in public'
(quoted, Heer, 1962, p. 317). And Aquinas described woman as 'a
necessary object. . . who is needed to preserve the species or to provide
food and drink'. Worse – woman was Eve, the receptacle of sin.

In terms of active involvement in their societies, in the early medieval
centuries, some women were prominent in trade and the crafts, areas of
activity which later became regulated by the guilds. That was the rub. As
we have recorded in Chapter Two, citizenship was municipal citizenship
and municipal citizenship was tightly bound to guild membership.
Women were excluded from these male fraternities; women were
accordingly excluded from any form of citizenship. Though, in truth,
there is little evidence that women had supported the burghers in their
struggle for civic freedom.

The possible right of women to vote in national elections in the
medieval and early-modern periods was an issue only in England. The
franchise (especially in boroughs) was notoriously vague and confused.
One consideration was none the less clear: that voting rights were
dependent upon property ownership. Married women had no property;
it was their husband's. But what about property-owning widows and
abbesses whose religious houses possessed considerable real estate?
There are, in fact, instances even of women, being the sole freeholders,
nominating MPs; and as late as the reign of James I an unmarried woman
with adequate property qualifications was judged to have a valid right
to vote; though that was revoked by the distinguished jurist Sir Edward
Coke in 1644.

The English Civil War intensified political debate, and it would be
surprising if women made no attempt to be involved. The most famous
incident occurred in 1649 when a group of women 'inhabiting the City
of London, Westminster, the Borough of Southwark, Hamblets (sic)

and places adjacent to the House of Commons' presented a Petition demanding the release from prison of the Leveller John Lilburne and his companions, and the redress of sundry grievances against Cromwell's government. The Petition argued that since 'we are assured of our creation in the image of God, and of an interest in Christ equal unto men', they had a right 'also of a proportionate share in the freedom of this Commonwealth' (quoted, Fraser, 1984, p. 269).

Nevertheless, all this was very tentative compared with American women's patriotic rallying to the cause of the Revolution and the political consciousness aroused in women's minds by the French Revolution and its proclamation of the rights of man and the citizen. Women played some dramatic roles in the French Revolution: for instance, the (albeit misleadingly named) 'March of the Women' to Versailles in October 1789 to drag the royal family to residence in Paris; the formidable Mme Roland, the politically active wife of the 'Girondin' minister; Charlotte Corday, the assassin of Marat; and the *tricoteuses* gloating over the dispatch of counter-revolutionaries by Dr Guillotin's machine.

More placidly, French women started to campaign for women's rights. In 1790 a group organized the *Cercle social* for this purpose. Most famous – or notorious in the eyes of many men – the self-styled Olympe de Gouge, pamphleteer and playwright, produced in 1791 a pamphlet, *The Declaration of the Rights of Woman*. This made the point that women should be treated as the equals of men by closely mirroring the language of the Declaration of the Rights of Man. A few of the articles illustrate this:

1. Woman is born free and equal to man in rights. . . .

3. The principle of all sovereignty rests essentially in the nation, which is but the reuniting of woman and man. . . .

6. All citizenesses and citizens, being equal in [the law's] eyes, should be equally admissible to all public dignities, offices, and employments. . . .

10. Woman has the right to mount the scaffold, so she should have the right equally to mount the tribune. (quoted, Hunt, 1996, p. 125)

Article 10 had a certain black prescience: de Gouge did mount the scaffold, in 1793, executed as a counter-revolutionary and an unnatural woman.

By this time women's clubs had sprung up throughout France, for charitable work and to help the war effort as well as to act as pressure groups. Despite their revolutionary patriotism, they were not tolerated by the male Jacobin politicians. A comment by the fearsome agent of the Terror, Amar, seems almost as though he were quoting Aristotle. He declared: 'In general, women are hardly capable of lofty conceptions and serious cogitations' (quoted, Hunt, 1996, p. 137). This was in October 1793; four days later de Gouge was executed. All women's clubs were banned.

The effects of the French Revolution were not confined to France. A year after de Gouge published her pamphlet Mary Wollstonecraft, a member of the English radical circle, published her very much more substantial *Vindication of the Rights of Woman*, the earliest major feminist work. In this book she exposed the persistent dilemma of moderate feminists, namely, how to manage simultaneously a public, civic life with domestic and familial duties when the husband is a fully-employed bread-winner.

In her book Wollstonecraft attempts to resolve this difficulty by envisaging a distinct and practicable civic role for women – a seemingly minor, though, she protests, an equal one to that pursued by men. She projects her imagination into the future,

> supposing that society will some time or other be so constituted, that man must necessarily fulfil the duties of a citizen, or be despised, and that while he was employed in any of the departments of civil life, his wife, also an active citizen, should be equally intent to manage her family, educate her children, and assist her neighbours.

She does not, however, leave it there; she continues:

> But to render her really virtuous and useful, she must not, if she discharge her civil duties, want individually the protection of civil laws; she must not be dependent on her husband's bounty for her subsistence during his life, or support after his death.   (Wollstonecraft, 1975, pp. 258–9)

The rational pleas of neither de Gouge nor Wollstonecraft could penetrate the male assumptions – prejudices, if you prefer – of the age, which, indeed, lingered for many decades: French women did not receive the vote until a century-and-a-half after de Gouge's pamphlet; English wives were unable to retain their own property until nearly a century after Wollstonecraft's book. Indeed, another half-century or more elapsed from the excitement of the revolutionary 1790s before the rights of women again became a live issue and an era of women's enfranchisement dawned.

The beginning of rights

The right to vote, a simple but key indicator of citizenship, was first allotted to New Zealand women in 1893. In contrast, a century later, in 1999, the Kuwaiti parliament, the only elected assembly in the Gulf, rejected a proposal to give women full political rights in 2003. The securing of women's civic rights has clearly been a lengthy process, and one that is as yet incomplete.

In addition to New Zealand, a few other states with small populations gave women the vote before the First World War – Australia, Finland, Norway and some of the constituent states of the USA. Of the major states, it was the USA and Britain where the vanguard movements for women's rights of citizenship made particularly early and effective starts in the nineteenth century.

The public activism of American women, mainly of middle-class standing, developed in several waves. The Revolution acted as a powerful stimulus. Then, from 1800 to 1830 came the Second Great Awakening, when women provided significant momentum to the religiously based complaints against the process of industrialization. Campaigning for the abolition of slavery followed, from the 1840s. In 1848 a group issued a Declaration of Sentiments, to which we shall return. After the Civil War, many women organized themselves for social activities, as 'social auxiliaries' and as campaigners for temperance, for example. And from the experience gained in the temperance movement there arose nationwide agitation for female suffrage, which became particularly demanding from *c*.1890.

To return to the Declaration of Sentiments. Two leading activists in the movement to abolish slavery were Lucretia Mott and Elizabeth Cady Stanton. Frustrated by the politically muted voices of women in this campaign, they determined to press for women's suffrage. Stanton lived in Seneca Falls in upstate New York, and at the Wesleyan Chapel there she convened a meeting of some 200 women to draft a campaigning document.

Just as Olympe de Gouge echoed the French Declaration of Rights, so the Seneca Falls Declaration of Sentiments echoed the American Declaration of Independence, in a tone of some bitterness, as these extracts reveal:

We hold these truths to be self-evident: that all men and women are created equal. . . . The history of mankind is the history of repeated injuries and usurpations on the part of man toward woman. . . . He has never permitted her to exercise her inalienable right to the elective franchise. He has compelled her to submit to laws, in the formation of which she has no voice. He has withheld from her rights which are given to the most ignorant and degraded men – both natives and foreigners. . . . Now. . . because women do feel themselves aggrieved, oppressed and fraudulently deprived of their most sacred rights, we insist that they have immediate admission to all the rights and privileges which belong to them as citizens of the United States. (quoted, Beard and Beard, 1944, p. 517)

Immediate success for Elizabeth Cady Stanton and her colleagues came in that same year when the state of New York passed its Married Women's Property Law. Other states followed suit. Because of America's federal Constitution reforms could occur in this piece-meal fashion; thus it was also with women's franchise. Wyoming territory led the way as early as 1869, followed by ten other states from 1893 to 1914.

These reforms were not a little due to the suffragist movements, of which there were two until their merger in 1890. The more combatant of the two was led by Susan B. Anthony, the doyenne of women's public activities, having been involved in the abolitionist and temperance movements as well as those for women's rights. So distinguished was her contribution to the women's cause, indeed, that when female suffrage was written into the Constitution in 1920 by the Nineteenth Amendment, it was dubbed the 'Susan Anthony Amendment'.

As in the United States, so in England, women active in the public arena variously and overlappingly campaigned for improvement in social conditions, for access to higher education, for entry into the professions as well as for civil and political rights; though, compared with their transatlantic sisters and despite Mary Wollstonecraft's path-breaking book, campaigning did not effectively get under way until the mid-nineteenth century or later. For over a quarter of a century Barbara Leigh Smith (Mme Bodichon) worked tirelessly for legal reform, her efforts crowned with success with the Married Women's Property Act in 1882.

Women's suffrage became a serious issue in the 1860s. When, in 1866, the Liberals introduced a Reform Bill for the extension of the franchise, a committee presented to the House of Commons an impressively supported petition for the inclusion of women. John Stuart Mill, at the time and briefly (1865–68) an MP, supported the amendment in the debate the next year. It failed, of course; to the accompaniment, it must be said, of some acid comments.

Mill was already, in fact, deeply committed to the cause: in 1861 he had written his forceful and clearly logical essay on *The Subjection of Women*, though he did not publish it until 1869. With Wollstonecraft's

Vindication it rates as one of the most compelling early arguments for women's rights, if not of all time. He states quite bluntly that 'the legal subordination of one sex to the other. . . is wrong in itself, and now one of the chief hindrances to human improvement' (Mill, 1911, p. 29).

English women were able actively to participate in local affairs before they achieved the national franchise. In the 1870s and 1880s they became members of School Boards, Poor Law Guardians and Parish Councillors. However, for many, nothing short of the national franchise would suffice. Suffrage societies sprang up, amalgamating as the National Union of Women's Suffrage Societies (NUWSS), a leading light in which was Millicent Fawcett. Their tame tactics achieving no results against entrenched male opposition, a more militant organization was founded in 1903 by Emmeline Pankhurst and her daughter Christabel, influenced by a speech in Manchester by Susan B. Anthony. This new body was called the Women's Social and Political Union (WSPU). The members were called 'suffragettes'.

From 1906 to 1914 especially, the inventive and courageous actions of the suffragettes to bring their cause to public notice gripped the nation's attention. Then, during the Great War, so many women proved their worth fulfilling 'men's' work – in order to release the young male part of the population for combat – that it was impossible to deny female suffrage any longer. In 1918 women over 30 were given the vote, then in 1928, those over 21.

Even so, British women continued to suffer many civil disabilities and much discrimination. Consequently, under the leadership of Eleanor Rathbone, the NUWSS transformed itself into the Union for Equal Citizenship. But it is not only British women who have been unequal citizens. Taking a world perspective, the task of achieving justice for women had scarcely begun.

The continuing problems

Even in Europe some states were extraordinarily laggard in enfranchising women, as these dates indicate: France, 1946; Switzerland, 1971. The right to vote is, of course, a milestone; but the journey to full citizenship needs to continue to achieve adequate representation in legislative assemblies and governments, to ensure equal employment opportunities, and to be protected from the myriad forms of male dominance and oppression. To take one example of variations in women's enjoyment of full citizenship: in 1999 40 per cent of the Swedish parliament were women, while the proportion in Greece was 6 per cent.

When, in the 1990s, democratic regimes succeeded Communist rule in the Soviet Union and eastern Europe and dictatorships in some Latin American and African states, the question arose, What about the place of women? The Russian women's movement coined the slogan, 'Democracy minus women is not democracy' (quoted, Ichilov, 1998, p.174). The maxim was taken up beyond Russia.

Already, from the 1960s, feminist movements and thinking burgeoned in the western world in a 'second wave' of demands for changes in women's place in the identity and role of citizenship. Not that these demands composed a unified programme. We may discern three main positions through the ages.

One is that women should be excluded from citizenship altogether as being unsuited by nature for the function: Aristotle's attitude. The polar opposite is that there should be no distinction between men and women: Mill's attitude. The third position is the most interesting: it is sometimes referred to as the concept of 'republican motherhood'. Republican motherhood was a much supported ideal from the eighteenth century, especially in the USA. Whereas the basic civic republican theory cast the role of the male as operating in the public sphere and the female, in the totally separate private sphere, republican motherhood portrayed women as having the vital citizenly role of bridging the two spheres. This could be achieved through activities which they have natural aptitudes to perform.

For all his prejudices against women, Rousseau hinted at this principle. Men, he believed, can be good citizens only if they live in a domestic environment conducive to the growth and maintenance of civic virtue. He asked:

> Can devotion to the state exist apart from the love of those near and dear to us? Can patriotism thrive except in the soil of that miniature fatherland, the home?   (Rousseau, 1911, p. 326)

Wollstonecraft also was beginning to develop her thoughts along these lines.

By the nineteenth century, this ideal had broadened in the United States to a whole panoply of women's civically virtuous activities: cultivating moral and patriotic mentalities in the younger generation; undertaking good works in the neighbourhood through individual, club or church initiatives; and participating in pressure groups at the local level for social and moral reform. If women conscientiously engaged in these responsibilities, was this not citizenship? And if they did, would they have the time to perform the male-devised forms of citizenship?

This latter question lay behind a notable US Supreme Court ruling in 1961 on the distinction made by the state of Florida between obligatory jury-service for men and voluntary service for women. The judgment ran:

> woman is still regarded as the center of home and family life. We cannot say that it is constitutionally impermissible for a State, acting in pursuit of the general welfare, to conclude that a woman should be relieved from the civic duty of jury service unless she herself determines that such service is consistent with her own special responsibilities. (quoted, Ichilov, 1998, p. 179)

Since the 1960s feminist arguments have followed three main courses. First is the continued pursuit of the liberal case for civil and political equality with men. The second is the socialist case, bolstered by the interpretation of Marx and Engels that the economy and the family have been male-dominated. This has led to a concentration on demands for equal opportunities in the work-place and improved state support for family-rearing. The third argument has been the suggestion that citizenship itself should be radically transformed, so that the quintessentially feminine contributions of caring – for the family, for the neighbourhood, for the environment – may be integral features of the identity and status.

We must not forget, however, that these programmes have been devised mainly by middle-class women living in the relatively affluent western world. For the large populations of women living in the still sternly patriarchal societies, no citizenly autonomy can be envisaged. For the hundreds of millions of poverty-stricken women in the underdeveloped countries, citizenship in whatever form is still a conceptual luxury of which they are either ignorant or which they cannot afford to contemplate in the daily grind of striving to survive.

Civic socialization and education

Framework of development

Many political theorists and governments alike have understood the need to strengthen, forge even, the links that bind and commit the citizen to the state and each other. Greeks and Romans had their civic religions, and Machiavelli and Rousseau were convinced of the efficacy of such arrangements. Rousseau also advocated the use of public gatherings and spectacles to foster civic concord and fraternity. He suggested a simple device:

> Plant a stake crowned with flowers in the middle of a square; gather the people together there, and you will have a festival. . . do it so that each [spectator] sees and loves himself in the others so that all will be better united.   (quoted, Oldfield, 1990, p. 72)

The French Revolutionaries took the lesson to heart: they planted trees of liberty; they also organized highly dramatic spectacles, notably the Fête of the Federation in 1790 to mark the anniversary of the fall of the Bastille and Robespierre's Fête of the Supreme Being, stage-managed by David, in 1794.

Totalitarian governments of the twentieth century developed civic spectacle to a fine art, especially the Nazi regime in Germany, where the programme was master-minded by the National Ministry of Propaganda and People's Enlightenment, the new medium of film being exploited with great skill. Two questions naturally arise from these techniques. First, if a people of a state are aroused to enthusiastic civic loyalty by manipulation of this kind, are they really behaving as true citizens? Surely citizenship requires the exercise of autonomous judgment. Secondly, since similar policies have been used in schools, as they certainly were in Nazi Germany, Stalinist Russia and Maoist China, is not that mode of teaching indoctrination, not education for free citizenship? Which brings us to the central issue of this section, namely, the role of schools in producing citizens.

Some of the greatest political thinkers were very conscious of the political importance of education: the ideas of Plato, Aristotle and Rousseau have already been touched upon in Chapters One and Four. The English and American Revolutions also prompted some consideration of the need for civic education – Winstanley, Hobbes and Jefferson, for example, expressed their ideas on the subject.

However, the first really concentrated thinking in modern times did not occur until after 1762, and this happened in France. In that year the doctrines of the Jesuits were declared 'pernicious to civil society, seditious, a challenge to the rights of the nation and royal authority' (quoted, Cobban, 1957, p. 86). The Society was abolished, its property was confiscated and the work of its members ceased – including teaching. The need arose to recruit other teachers and the opportunity was given to propound the possibility of a secular education for French children. Since the state and not the Church would be the providing authority, one corollary was that religious objectives would be replaced by political. Conditions were in fact ripe for taking advantage of this sudden collapse of Jesuit power. The philosophes, notably Helvétius, were already expounding the advantage of an educational system with a civic purpose.

The campaign against the Society of Jesus was spearheaded by the *parlements*, the politically ambitious high courts. The senior lawyer, *procureur-général*, of the *parlement* of Rennes was La Chalotais, who was rarely temperate in his political activities, and was passionately hostile to the Jesuits. In 1762 he produced his *Essay on National Education*. He advocated state control of education, which made his work widely read, and civic education for the privileged classes, which makes it relevant for our purposes. The more attractive personality, Turgot, the provincial administrator and economist, proposed a Council of Public Instruction, the responsibilities of which would have included the compilation of textbooks on the duties of citizenship. Less well-known men added their support for the basic idea of state-controlled education with civic instruction. One, Navarre, bewailed the absence of civic purpose in the traditional curriculum: 'Why should not literary education serve to multiply among our youth the prodigy of political virtues?' he asked (quoted, Palmer, 1940, p. 101).

These aims were absorbed into public consciousness, to emerge, as we have seen in Chapter Four, as one of the most common demands in the *cahiers* of 1789. In 1792 a thorough and systematic report was compiled by the philosopher-politician Condorcet for a national system of education suited to the new era, *An Education for Democracy*. He was quite adamant that 'moral and political sciences should be an essential part of political education', for,

A people will never enjoy an assured and permanent freedom, if education in political science is not general, if it is not independent of all social institutions, if the enthusiasm which you stir in the hearts of citizens is not directed by reason.   (Condorcet, 1982, pp. 184, 185)

Yet for all this convinced opinion over a period of thirty years that French education should be restyled, nothing was at that time accomplished in practice. It was left to the United States to pioneer modern state and civic education.

During the second half of the nineteenth century and throughout the twentieth, programmes of education for citizenship fell into two main categories: those designed to shape the minds of pupils for political and social purposes, and those designed to encourage pupils to think for themselves about political and social issues.

It is possible to discern three intentions in the first category. One is the political conformity model. This has involved teaching about the state's constitution and its positive qualities, and the country's history with an emphasis on events conducive to a feeling of patriotic pride. The second is the use of schools to cement a sense of national unity and identity. The third intention is to support the social *status quo*; though, since states are neither politically nor socially static, the history of citizenship education reveals constant adaptations to accommodate these changes. The three different intentions may be exemplified respectively as follows: the American and French courses teaching about their republican and constitutional traditions; the efforts of the US also to use its schools as instruments for national cohesion; and the effect of the division in England between the Public (i.e. private) and state sectors of education in undergirding social divisions, and the efforts by German teachers constantly to adapt to changing political conditions and pedagogical fashions.

The second category embraces the ways in which the teaching profession has tried to liberate citizenship education from these constrained, even indoctrinatory policies. During the twentieth century and with growing impetus since the 1960s the subject-content of teaching for citizenship expanded geographically beyond the pupil's state and its political system. Teaching about the League of Nations and the United Nations and the need for peace, about human rights, about global environmental stresses stretched some syllabuses into education for world citizenship. Another variation has concerned the teaching objectives: less concentration on facts, more on developing judgment; less concentration on national pride, more on developing critical faculties.

Nor have moves away from or supplements to traditional styles of citizenship education been confined to the classroom curriculum. As an essential facet of citizenship is a sense of responsibility for the condition of our fellow-citizens, so preparation for that adult status has come to include practical, helpful community work. This approach reflects a recognition that citizenship involves attitudes as well as knowledge and skills. And attitudes are caught as much as they are taught. Therefore, if modern citizenship exists and is exercised in an essentially democratic context, then pupils, so some have argued, should grow up in a democratic educational environment. The most distinguished exponent of this argument was the American educational philosopher John Dewey. Teachers' respect for pupils' opinions; school councils; classroom discussion, where appropriate, rather than 'full-frontal' (the term is Professor Ian Lister's) didactic teaching – all have been advocated and used to provide an ethos or a 'hidden curriculum' germane to citizenship as responsibility and participation.

Examples of policies and practices

To illustrate differences in the ways countries have, in modern times, implemented education for citizenship, the approaches of the USA, France and England will be summarized in this section.

The United States provides a clear example of both the political conformity and national cohesion models, responses to the republican democratic ideal and then the immigrant 'melting-pot' process respectively. By the 1840s courses in Civics were well established in American elementary and secondary schools. In 1916 'Social Studies' was formally adopted as a portmanteau term for the Civics, Geography and History components of the curriculum. The civic purpose underlying Social Studies has always been a major part of their rationale.

Because of the devolution of school policy to the state level and, even more, to the school districts – of which there were at the turn of the twentieth century over 15,000 – it is difficult in some ways to describe the detail of American citizenship education. Even so, there has been a remarkably uniform general pattern. One authority, writing in 1931, explained:

> America has laid great stress upon the value of the school. . . as a democratic agency. . . . There has developed a large amount of formal training not alone in the history of the republic but also in civics or civil government. In many states this has been made obligatory by legislative act, and where there has been no such law, great emphasis has been placed on this form of education. . . . In no other country has there been a more elaborate development of this particular form of civic training in its formal outlines.   (Merriam, 1966, p. 252)

The catch was in that penultimate word: the author was less impressed by the quality of this teaching, describing many of the courses as 'superficial and formal'.

Meanwhile, the progressive education movement was refashioning Social Studies in some schools, encouraging analysis, reasoning and activity rather than rote learning. Dewey's work and his book *Democracy and Education* (1916) were influential. Yet, for the most part, little changed. The ineffectualness of Social Studies teaching generated caustic criticism and a flurry of curriculum reform in the 1960s. The result has been summed up in the following words: 'To assert that social studies was in disarray in the early years of the 1970s would be a generous assessment of the situation' (Jarolimek, 1981, p. 9). Concerning the situation twenty years later, two other experienced authorities judged that 'There is a deep malaise in citizenship education' (Ichilov, 1998, p.99). *Plus ça change...*!

Little wonder, then, that increasing faith was being placed in school activities: rituals like the daily salute to the flag, pupil participation in school councils and organization of school clubs, already evident in the early years of the twentieth century.

The histories of education for citizenship in the USA and France share significant attributes. Each country has been extremely keen to instil into its young people a pride in the democratic traditions of the republic, America since *c.*1800, France since *c.*1880; and each has had to face up to the school's contribution to the assimilation of immigrants, America from the late nineteenth century, France from the late twentieth century.

History does not repeat itself, though one could be forgiven a *déjà vu* experience when comparing French interest in civic education in the 1760s and 1880s. For, just as plans followed the dispersal of members of the Society of Jesus in the earlier period, so an actual requirement to include this teaching followed the second dispersal of the Jesuits (they were restored in 1814) in 1880.

The latter attack on their pedagogical role was instigated by Jules Ferry, who was determined to secularize French education, make attendance at elementary school mandatory and to place '*l'instruction civique*' firmly in the curriculum. These objectives he achieved in 1882. Moreover, since, in complete contradistinction from the USA, the French school system was highly centralized, the minister could command what was taught in all state schools. Ferry duly dispatched an outline syllabus. The teachers' function was to be 'a natural aid to moral and social progress'; their task, 'to prepare a generation of good citizens for our country' (quoted, Thomson, 1958, p. 145).

The tone of what was required was lucidly explained in the 1911 edition of the *Dictionnaire Pedagogie*, which defined the principles of national policy in these words:

> to instill into [children] the respect for all the traditions worthy of it, while at the same time imprinting on their minds the meaning of progress. . . to enable them to acknowledge. . . what the new [i.e. post-1789] system has done for the happiness and honor of the Nation; to familiarize them with the tenets of the Revolution of 1789. . . to familiarize them with the fundamental rules of the division

of power. . . to teach this. . . means preparing children to love their country, to abide by its laws, to respect its government, to exercise all their rights, to carry out all their obligations as citizens, above all, their civic rights and duties.   (quoted, Carduner, 1987, pp. 91–2)

All these aims were to be achieved in the main by the judicious selection of teaching material from the nation's history. Surveying the scene some two decades later, an American authority assessed the French system of civic education as having a 'uniformity and thoroughness' probably unequalled anywhere else; and, moreover '*La France* emerges from these studies, regnant and serene' (Merriam, 1966, pp. 133, 127).

From 1945, however, matters became more complicated. Syllabus content changed, disagreements erupted concerning the most appropriate and up-to-date content and teaching methodologies, and the relative cultural homogeneity of the student population was weakened by immigration, especially of Muslims. Moreover civic education remained a somewhat staid, classroom-bound process, lacking the modern American feeling of schools as micro-communities preparing their embryo-citizens for adult civic participation.

Compared with the deep commitment and tight central government control in the French Third Republic, the English government during the same period, and beyond, evinced little interest and was charged with little control in any case. An Education Minister declared as late as 1999: 'we are alone among our European partners and a great many other developed countries in not having a formal citizenship education in the curriculum' (Hansard, 1999, col. 460). This is one of several features in English history that have helped shape civic education in that country. The others are social class distinctions, extension of the franchise, war and consciousness of Empire.

During the reign of Elizabeth I the Privy Council ordered the bishops to have a textbook entitled *De Proeliis Anglorum* read in the schools: the story of England's prowess in war would, it was thought, boost the pupils' sense of patriotism. But not until 2000 did an English government announce that citizenship education would be a required part of the curriculum. Insofar as teaching of this kind was undertaken in the nineteenth and twentieth centuries, it resulted from limited guidelines from central government, the enthusiasm of teachers and the assistance of professional organizations (e.g. the Association for Education in Citizenship (1935–1957), the Citizenship Foundation (from 1989)).

The co-existence of the state and so-called Public schools, which helped so signally to keep the upper and working classes apart, ensured that two distinct strands of civic training evolved in England in the nineteenth century. The one system was designed to produce a submissive proletariat through moralizing injunctions from the teachers about work, loyalty and temperance; the other, a governing elite educated in the Classics. So oppressive was the atmosphere in the state Board Schools that one commentator was moved to a mood of wonder in 1894, declaring: 'it is nothing short of marvellous that any of the pupils, when they become adults, break away from the old rut of submissive obedience' (Hobart, 1894, n.p.).

When some of the artisan class were enfranchised in 1867 and the Board Schools were created after 1870, the need to educate these additions to the electorate was acknowledged – but it was basic literacy that the advocates had in mind. Political education was often considered beyond the comprehension of adolescents and, probably, undesirable. However, after 1969 everyone had the vote from the age of 18, and in 1972 the minimum school-leaving age was raised to 16. Henceforth, a mere two years separated the school-pupil from full citizen status. Teachers and even a few politicians thought it appropriate to provide civic education, though implementation was slow.

Our survey thus far has related to the induction of young people into their own societies. Yet citizenship can be conceived, as we saw in Chapter Five, in an international or world sense as well. American and English teachers from the inter-War years and French teachers after the Second World War introduced this dimension into their syllabuses. The critical problems of the Cold War and the global environment reinforced the relevance, though also the contentiousness, of a world perspective. The two World Wars and the existence of nuclear weapons prompted the teaching of what came to be called Peace Studies.

In England teachers had an additional consideration and extra subject-matter to take into account, namely, the existence and then the legacy of the British Empire and Commonwealth. So lessons encouraging chauvinistic pride, and subsequently an understanding of Britain as a multicultural nation entered the schools.

Effect of political change

Few states can have undergone so many changes of regime, and, in the process, experienced such deeply felt alterations in the style of government – and, as a consequence, of citizenship education – as Germany over the past two centuries. From the era of the French Revolution to the Franco–Prussian War, the desire for national unity was frustrated. From 1871 to 1918 Germany was a Hohenzollern Empire. From 1918 to 1933 it was a democratic federal republic. From 1933 to 1945, a Nazi totalitarian regime. From 1945 to 1990, partitioned between the western democratic Federal Republic of Germany and the Communist German Democratic Republic. And since 1990 the FRG has been striving to incorporate the former Communist *Länder* (states).

In the winter of 1807–8 Fichte delivered his *Addresses to the German Nation* in Berlin, at that time under occupation by Napoleon's army, following Prussia's military defeat. His nationalist message contained a strong educational thread: 'the majority of citizens,' he declared, 'must be educated to [a] sense of fatherland. . . education is the sole means of saving German independence' (Fichte, 1968, p. 132). In another text he asserted that the 'sacred duty of all schoolmasters and mistresses' was to make every Prussian school 'a nursery of blameless patriotism' (quoted, Wilds and Lottich, 1970, p. 326). The nationalist purpose persisted through the nineteenth century, for example, in Bismarck's policy of wresting control of schools from the Catholic Church and imposing state control.

After the First World War, the Weimar Republic, while rejecting the authoritarianism of nineteenth-century Germany, accepted both its federal structure and its belief in the political purpose of education. Civic education was even written into its constitution (Article 148):

> In all schools effort shall be made to develop moral education, civic sentiments, and personal and vocational efficiency, in the spirit of the German national character and of international conciliation.   (quoted, Merriam, 1966, p. 127, n.7)

All the states of the federation, but especially Prussia, placed considerable emphasis on a patriotic reverence for the German republic.

The accession to power of the National Socialist government brought radical changes. In 1933 Guiding Principles for School Organization were framed. A raft of regulations was put into effect which revolutionized the school curriculum, the textbooks used and the ethos of the school, all for the political purpose of inculcating Nazi beliefs and behaviour. Academic studies were subordinated to 'character training'. The opportunity for school pupils to learn to think independently about political matters became for all intents and purposes non-existent.

Whether from conviction or in order to safeguard their careers, a large proportion of teachers became members of the Nazi Party; and because of similar social pressures, young people joined the youth movements whose indoctrinatory programmes reinforced the messages transmitted in the schools. Children were therefore trained to be good citizens of the Third Reich; but only in the Aristotelean sense of being matched to the state's system of government, not in the liberal sense of developing the faculty of judgment.

Immediately after the defeat of Germany in 1945, the Allied occupation powers faced the task of denazification. Schools had to be provided with new textbooks; teachers with a virulent Nazi past had to be dismissed, though replacements were hard to find. When the FRG and GDR emerged as consolidated states from the occupation zones, the new policies for civic education were very easily defined in this negative sense of obliterating the Nazi interlude. Nevertheless, whereas a reformed style of teaching was quickly and simply defined in a positive sense in the GDR, in the FRG an equivalent positive policy proved tantalizingly elusive.

In the GDR, courses in Marxism-Leninism were made compulsory at all levels in the education system, and the work of the schools in shaping good, young loyal socialists was supported by the Free German Youth: modes of indoctrination very reminiscent of the Nazis' methods, though without their racist intent.

Meanwhile, in West Germany the *leitmotiv* was the teaching of the evils of Nazism in contrast to the task of creating a new democratic polity. One schoolbook, published in 1961, bore the telling title, *Hitler: A Report for Young Citizens*. Yet a concerted programme for all schools during the second half of the twentieth century was difficult to achieve for a number of reasons. The federal constitutional system precluded a state-wide syllabus; fluctuating educational theories influenced some teachers to change their primary objectives and teaching methods; and no co-ordinated policy emerged concerning the respective roles of traditional subjects, especially History, and Social Studies. One German authority, writing in the 1980s, declared that,

> Political education is believed to be in a crisis. The subject is drifting increasingly into isolation with a growing tendency to be incorporated in the subject history. The [social] scientists and educationists dealing with political education are partly to be blamed.   (Meyenberg, 1990, p. 216)

By the end of the century, nevertheless, discernible patterns were emerging, using a mixture of History and Social Studies (including discussion of current affairs), the most common pedagogical technique being the delineation of arguments for and against a particular policy or condition.

As these solutions to the problem of citizenship education were evident in the schools, another issue had arisen, namely the incorporation of the former GDR *Länder* into the Federal Republic. Harmonizing citizenly attitudes across the reunified state, inevitably, proved to be a difficult task. In the first place, East Germans were poorer. Secondly, having lived under totalitarian regimes for 57 years, they had been used to an authoritarian mode of government and had become cynical about politics. Thirdly, poverty and lack of a tradition of tolerance have inhibited the growth of the give-and-take sense of responsibility upon which the citizenship ethic rests. Both politicians and educationists were determined to use the schools to promote a sense of democratic citizenship, though a relatively slow process it was assuredly to be.

In all countries, devising suitable forms of citizenship education that avoid indoctrination has proved to be not an easy operation. Through lack of agreement or commitment among educationists or lack of political will-power in governments, the great effort needed to overcome the difficulties has only slowly and partially been forthcoming. Furthermore, where and when praiseworthy efforts have been made, it has become obvious that schools are not operating in a vacuum. If messages of apathy, cynicism and alienation are sent to young people from other influences such as parents, peers, pop-culture and the mass-media, then the schools have the enormous extra job of overcoming these negative signals before any positive teaching can have a chance of taking effect. This is a prominent item on schools' agendas for the twenty-first century, and one which, if effectively handled, could influence the quality of citizenship itself in that new era.

Conclusion

Dilemmas in historical context

While dismissing the sceptic's adage that the only thing we can learn from history is that we can learn nothing from history, it is none the less necessary to beware the simplistic contrary notion that history repeats itself. Let us adopt as our guideline rather the assertion of the distinguished Swiss historian Herbert Lüthy that, 'Consciousness of the past alone can make us understand the present'. So, taking our stance at the beginning of the twenty-first century, it is useful to ask how a consciousness of the nature of citizenship in the past – for all its transmogrifications over the centuries – can illuminate its condition now.

In the Introduction we noted Peter Riesenberg's portrayal of the history of citizenship as revealing the highlights of a series of 'perfect moments'. At the start of the twenty-first century we have arrived not so much at a perfect moment, but instead at a moment of quandary. In which ways should citizenship be developed and encouraged? We are really not at all sure. We are, in fact, faced with four basic dilemmas, three relatively straightforward to examine, the other, exceedingly complex.

These problems exercise the minds of political and social theorists and present politicians with the need to make practical policy choices. As a study of history reveals, none of these dilemmas is unique to our own age, though there are unique features to their expression today. One, obviously, is that the resolution of the dilemmas can only be achieved by reference to the particular current conditions: no use looking to the Greeks, Romans or French Revolutionaries, for instance, because they faced up to these issues in accordance with their own particular conditions. The other unique feature today is that, unlike any other period in history, theoretical and practical discussions are being conducted in a more intense manner and in a more truly global arena than ever before. Yet, however intractable the dilemmas we have identified may appear to be, an appreciation that they have historical lineages and parallels may be some comfort: in the great span of the recorded history of citizenship, we are not alone in having to tussle with these matters, albeit in our own ways.

The first dilemma is how to strike a balance between duties and rights. How different were the visions of citizenship in this regard as described by Lycurgus and Marshall, for example. And in the modern drafting of constitutions we may cite the 1936 Soviet instrument and the 1996 South African as official documents that, although of markedly different provenance, consciously attempted to list these corresponding signifiers of the citizenly status.

The advance of the liberal version of citizenship with its stress on rights appeared to many observers in the twentieth century to have gone too far. The original focus on duties, responsibilities and obligations had been submerged. Yet, of course, to revoke the accumulated rights was and is unthinkable. The dilemma has been, instead, how to weave both strands into a holistic style of citizenship theory and practices. It is clear that, in order to accomplish this, the republican ideals of community and virtue must somehow be strengthened without undermining the rights of the individual. Words like 'reciprocity' and 'mutuality' have been used (e.g., Dagger, 1997; Parry, 1991) to conjure up a design of individuals recognizing the rights of others while enjoying their own, and recognizing, also, that rights can only exist in a communal context. But the practical implementation of such a design is no simple task.

The inherited struggle for priority – or hoped-for balance – between duties and rights is closely allied to the second dilemma, that is, how to achieve compatibility between civil and political citizenship on the one hand and social citizenship on the other. We have seen in Chapter Six how Marshall established the principle, now widely accepted, that citizenship cannot be a whole or completed status without the social element. Yet who is to gainsay the validity of one citizen protecting his or her property as a civic right by exercising the political right of voting against raising taxes to support the social conditions of another citizen?

Awareness of a longer and more varied history of the relationship between these components throws up other questions. To take two examples; and since neither feature in the above text, a little explanatory detail is needed here.

One question is whether social rights are given as entitlements, concessions or as a policy of prudence. If a government voluntarily gives social (including economic) rights as entitlements to all citizens, that is a recognition of these rights as components of true citizenship. If they are given only as concessions to ease the hardships of the poor, that is state charity. If they are given as a preventative of social upheaval, that is prudential conservation of social stability. The test of social citizenship, initially therefore, is the state's motive; though, true, once this arrangement is made it can harden into an accepted component of the citizen's status.

Our illustration of this question is taken from ancient Rome. In the second century BC the Gracchi brothers worked to introduce a number of reforms to benefit the poorer citizens, including land redistribution and subsidizing corn. That the land allocation was related to citizenship was made clear when peoples adjacent to Rome pressed for the status in order to qualify. But what of the motives of the Gracchi? Mainly to increase the power of the plebs vis-à-vis the elite – a strengthening of the egalitarian feature of citizenship.

The second question relates to this example, namely the causal connection between civil/political and social citizenship. The social reforms of the Gracchi helped accelerate the expansion of the number of people enjoying the legal status of Roman citizen. Another example poses the issue in another way. The nineteenth-century English Chartist movement was a demand for parliamentary reform. On the surface the Chartists were trying to improve the status of the unenfranchised. But not necessarily for its own political sake. One of the leaders declared the movement to be not so much a question of the ballot-box, but a knife-and-fork question: greater political influence by the population as a whole over the composition of the House of Commons would lead to reforms advancing the economic conditions of the unprivileged.

It is clear that the civil, political and social forms of citizenship cannot be compartmentalized: change in one sphere can well affect another. The problem is, how to relate them harmoniously.

The third dilemma concerns the most beneficial mix of participation in and abstinence from public affairs. At the end of the twentieth century many complaints were heard concerning disillusionment about, alienation from and apathy towards public affairs (see, e.g., Jowell and Park, 1998). Active citizenship, it is argued, is necessary for a healthy, well-ordered polity. Widespread negative attitudes are, therefore, unhealthy, dangerous even. Yet, at the other end of the spectrum from cold apathy is heated zealotry. 'The Revolution is frozen,' St Just complained, and the citizens of France had to be induced through the heat of the Terror to resume the hectic pace of change. So, again, how to animate a passive citizenry without provoking uncontrolled passion is a dilemma for the theorist even if civic fanaticism in practice in the modern world seems ages away in the eras of Nazism and the Chinese Red Guards.

Encouragement rather than enforcement is the accepted formula. The Athenians achieved it to a degree. Yet how can the sense of community possible in a *polis* be translated into a modern nation-state? Can cybernetics create a virtual *polis*? In 2003 a few citizens cast their votes in the extraordinary gubernatorial recall election in the US state of California by Touch Screen Voting (TSV) in the polling booths. The ultimate, however, is voting at home via the citizen's own computer. Nevertheless, if citizenship descends to merely pressing a few keys on a keyboard, is that not pandering to apathy?

The fourth and final dilemma is a paradox that strikes at the very heart of citizenship. Interest in the subject and status is now greater than it has been for some two hundred years or more; yet at the same time, it might appear to be disintegrating as a coherent concept for the twenty-first century.

One of the major reasons for the revitalization of citizenship in theory and practice in the late twentieth century was the enhanced consciousness of the value of democracy and its adoption as a style of government by an increasing number of countries. The status of citizen was in origin and indeed for by far the greatest portion of its history essentially the mark of an elite. The implication of the liberal revolution in the concept is that none should be excluded. It has usually been accepted as an objective, established by Sparta, that all citizens should be equal; therefore if all are citizens, all individuals should be equal. And since citizenship is a political status, the equality of citizens requires a democratic form of polity. If totalitarian regimes and military dictatorships based on powerful cadres exist, if certain segments of society even in liberal states are not treated equally – women and ethnic minorities, for instance – then true democracy and therefore universal citizenship do not prevail.

Towards the end of the twentieth century many authoritarian regimes were displaced by constitutional governments in Europe, Africa and Latin America. Furthermore, 'second-class' citizens in liberal states have successfully campaigned for equal rights. Citizenship, in a reasonably meaningful way, is, as a consequence, enjoyed by a larger proportion of the world's population than ever before.

Yet, alongside these signs of consolidation of citizenship, individuals are becoming increasingly conscious of their multiple identities, and the significance of the state, and of state citizenship, is declining. If people work in an environment of global networks of business or professional contacts; if families are deeply conscious of their religious beliefs and ethnic traditions disassociated from the mainstream culture of their country of residence; if women want to shape their lives and commitments in particular feminine ways – if developments such as these continue to burgeon, citizenship, which claims a cohering function, must either shrink to a weaker, because competing, form of allegiance among others, or expand to embrace them all and lose its coherence.

Moreover, the forces of globalization, sub-continental integration in Europe and regionalism are undermining the sovereign power and solidity of the state. Yet citizenship evolved in essence, pace medieval municipal citizenship, as a relationship of the individual to the state. If the state weakens so, ipso facto, does citizenship.

These considerations present a troublesome list of problems for resolution. We may identify three ways forward, for which there are interesting historical precedents. First, effective institutions to enable and encourage citizens to participate in their several citizenly guises must be made available. Secondly, there must be an acceptance that citizenship, however flexibly defined, is not the be-all and end-all of a person's social identity. And thirdly, individuals should be taught about their multiple identities and how to manage them compatibly.

The issue of institutions has a double aspect: the requirement that they be easily accessible at all levels from local community to world and that they be devised to handle matters of popular interest, e.g., environmental questions from the parochial to the global. On its own tiny scale, the Athenian civic structure as established by Cleisthenes achieved this; though the task today is, of course, incomparably more formidable.

Now to our second problem. In its main, basic sense, citizenship still involves living in and being committed to a nation-state, with the rights and duties prevailing in that form of polity. But, in addition, it is expected that the citizen should participate in some manner in the generally accepted culture of the community. All should be able to communicate in the country's main language or one of its main languages. All should be tolerant of the different religions, social habits and political beliefs that make up today's variegated countries – that is, modes of social identity outside citizenship. This means a recognition of 'horizontal' citizenship, the harmonious relationship between citizen and citizen, as well as between citizen and state: the Aristotelian concept of concord; the French Revolutionary concept of fraternity.

The Romans were quite successful in tackling this aspect of citizenship. As we have seen, the Roman citizenship was awarded throughout the Empire. Now, although there was no pressure to learn Latin, schools for teaching the language were well supported by the more affluent provincials. Also, apart from the difficulty Roman authorities had in accommodating Christianity, religious tolerance was the official policy. Consequently, citizens throughout the Empire could feel proud of and be committed to the Roman state without surrendering their local cultures.

However, the really difficult question is how the individual can cope with multiple social identities – family, religion, employment, let alone multiple political citizenship – state, European, world. We can gather two approaches from history. One is the Stoic position with regard to balancing state and world citizenship as thought through by Seneca and Marcus Aurelius. The other is the concept of concentric circles.

This notion has been remarkably persistent from the fourth century BC, when it was propounded by Theophrastus (Aristotle's successor as head of the Lyceum) to the present day. It pictures the individual as placed at the centre of a series of concentric circles representing social relationships – from the nearest (e.g., family) to the most remote (e.g., the world). The English poet Alexander Pope described the idea most graphically in his *Essay on Man* (quoted, Heater, 2002, pp. 49–50):

> God loves from whole to parts: but human soul
> Must rise from individual to the whole.
> Self-love but serves the virtuous mind to wake,
> As the small pebble stirs the peaceful lake;
> The centre moved, a circle straight succeeds,
> Another still, and still another spreads,
> Friend, parent, neighbour first it will embrace,
> His country next; and next all human race;
> Wide and more wide, the o'erflowings of the mind
> Take every creature in, of every kind;
> Earth smiles around, with boundless bounty blest,
> And Heaven beholds its image in his breast.

Many interpretations have been placed on the concentric circle theory, but all have incorporated relationships in addition to the specifically civic. One of the most important reasons for the differences is disagreement about the order of priority that should be accorded to the individual's various moral commitments. In citizenship terms, should citizens give a fuller commitment to their town or the world? And what about the intermediate circles, notably, it goes without saying, the state? These are issues that should be more widely understood and debated.

All the above considerations present a formidable list of dilemmas for resolution. None the less, the story told in this book is of a form of socio-political identity surviving from *c.*700 BC to AD 2000 by processes of continual metamorphosis. There is no reason why citizenship should not continue to adapt and survive.

References and Select Bibliography

Aristophanes (trans. and intro. D. Barrett), *The Frogs and Other Plays* (Harmondsworth, Penguin, 1964).

Aristotle (trans. and ed. E. Barker), *Politics* (Oxford, Clarendon Press, 1948).

Aristotle (trans. J.A.K. Thomson), *The Ethics of Aristotle* (Harmondsworth, Penguin, 1955).

Aristotle (trans. and intro. P.J. Rhodes), *The Athenian Constitution* (Harmondsworth, Penguin, 1984).

Bagley, J.J., *Historical Interpretation I: Sources of English Medieval History 1066–1540* (Harmondsworth, Penguin, 1965).

Beard, C.A. and M.R., *A Basic History of the United States* (New York, Doubleday, Doran & Co, 1944).

Beiner, R. (ed.), *Theorizing Citizenship* (Albany, NY, State University of New York Press, 1995).

Beloff, M., *The Debate on the American Revolution 1761–1783* (London, Nicholas Kaye, 1949).

Berki, R.N., *The History of Political Thought: A Short Introduction* (London, Dent and Totowa, NJ, Rowman & Littlefield, 1977).

Bonjour, E., Offler, H.S. and Potter, G.R., *A Short History of Switzerland* (Oxford, Clarendon Press, 1952).

Bouloiseau, M. *et al.* (eds), *Oeuvres de Maximilien Robespierre, vol. 9.* (Paris, Presses Universitaires de France, 1952).

Boyd, W., *The History of Western Education* (London, A. & C. Black, 3rd edn, 1932)

Brubaker. W.R., *Citizenship and Nationhood in France and Germany* (Cambridge MA, and London, Harvard University Press, 1992).

Bryce, J., *The Holy Roman Empire* (London, Macmillan and New York, St Martin's Press, 1968).

Bulmer, M. and Rees, A.M. (eds), *Citizenship Today: The Contemporary Relevance of T.H. Marshall* (London and Bristol, PA, University College London Press, 1966).

Burtt, S., *Virtue Transformed: Political Argument in England 1688–1740* (Cambridge, Cambridge University Press, 1992).

Carduner, J., 'The Making of French Citizens: Conflicts between Fading Traditions and Emerging Values' in E.B. Gumbert (ed.), *In the Nation's Image* (Atlanta, GA, Center for Cross-Cultural Education, Georgia State University, 1987).

Cartledge, P., *Sparta and Lakonia: A Regional History 1300–362 BC* (London, Routledge & Kegan Paul, 1979).

Chaffee, S.H., Morduchowicz, R. and Galperin, H., 'Education and Democracy in Argentina: Effects of a Newspaper-in-School Program' in Ichilov, O. (ed.) (1998).

Chandlet, J.M., *Life, Liberty and the Pursuit of Happiness* (London, Oxford University Press, 1971).

Cicero (trans. R. Gardner) 'Pro Balbo' in *The Speeches* (London, Heinemann and Cambridge, MA, Harvard University Press, 1958).

Clarke, P.B., *Citizenship* (London, Pluto Press, 1994).

Claussen, B. and Mueller, H. (eds), *Political Socialization of the Young in East and West* (Frankfurt am Main, Peter Lang, 1990).

Cloots, A., *Bases Constitutionnelles de la République du Genre Humain* (Paris, Convention Nationale, 1793).

Cobban, A., *A History of Modern France, Vol. 1* (Harmondsworth, Penguin, 1957).

Cobban, A., *Rousseau and the Modern State* (London, Allen & Unwin, 2nd edn, 1964).

Cobban, A., *Aspects of the French Revolution* (London, Cape, 1968).

Commission of the C.C. of the C.P.S.U. (B.), *History of the Communist Party of the Soviet Union (Bolsheviks)* (Moscow, Foreign Languages Publishing House, 1951).

Condorcet, Marquis de (ed. B. Backo), *Une Éducation pour la démocratie* (Paris, Éditions Garnier Frères, 1982).

Cowell, F.R., *Cicero and the Roman Republic* (London, Pitman, 1948).

Davis, G., *My Country is the World* (London, Macdonald, 1961).

Dawson, K. and Wall, P., *Society and Industry in the 19th Century: 1. Parliamentary Representation* (Oxford, Oxford University Press, 1968).

Dickinson, H.T., *Liberty and Property: Political Ideology in Eighteenth-century Britain* (London, Methuen, 1977).

Edmonds, J.M. (trans. and ed.), *Elegy and Iambus* (London, Heinemann and Cambridge, MA, Harvard University Press, 1961).

The Federalist 1787: various edns.

Fichte, J.G. (ed. G.A. Kelly), *Addresses to the German Nation* (New York, Harper & Row, 1968).

Forrest, W.G., *A History of Sparta 950–192 BC* (London, Hutchinson, 1968).

Forsyth, M., *Reason and Revolution: The Political Thought of the Abbé Sieyes* (Leicester, Leicester University Press and New York: Holmes & Meyer, 1987).

France, A. (trans. F. Davies), *The Gods Will Have Blood* (Harmondsworth, Penguin, 1979).

Fraser, A., *The Weaker Vessel* (London, Methuen, 1984).

Friedman, J.R., *Basic Facts on the Republic of South Africa and the Policy of Apartheid* (New York, United Nations, 1978).

Fukuyama, F., *The End of History and the Last Man* (Harmondsworth, Penguin, 1992).

Guardian 1998, 7 December.

Guardian 1999, 21 October.

Guiccardini, F. (ed. A. Brown), *Dialogue on the Government of Florence* (Cambridge, Cambridge University Press, 1994).

Habermas, J., 'Citizenship and National Identity' in van Steenbergen, B. (ed.), *The Condition of Citizenship* (London, Sage, 1994).

Hadow, W.H., *Citizenship* (Oxford, Clarendon Press, 1923).

Hahn, C.L., *Becoming Political: Comparative Perspectives in Citizenship Education* (Albany NY, State University of New York Press, 1998).

Hampson, N., *The Life and Opinions of Maximilien Robespierre* (London, Duckworth, 1974).

Hansard (House of Lords), 18 January 1999.

Hattersley, R. in *Guardian*, 6 December 1999.

Heater, D., *World Citizenship: Cosmopolitan Thinking and its Opponents* (London, Continuum, 2002).

Heater, D., *A History of Education for Citizenship* (Falmer, Routledge, 2003).

Heater, D., *Citizenship: The Civic Ideal in World History, Politics and Education* (Manchester, Manchester University Press, 3rd edn, 2004).

Heer, F., *The Medieval World* (London, New English Library, 1961).

Held, D., *Democracy and the Global Order* (Cambridge, Polity Press, 1991).

Herodotus (trans. A. de Selincourt), *The Histories* (Harmondsworth, Penguin, 1954).

Hobart, H.W. *Justice*, 30 June 1894.

Hunt, L. (ed., trans. and intro.), *The French Revolution and Human Rights: A Brief Documentary History* (New York, St Martin's Press, 1996).

Hyslop, B., *French Nationalism in 1789 according to the General Cahiers* (New York, Columbia University Press, 1934).

Ichilov, O. (ed.), *Citizenship and Citizenship Education in a Changing World* (London and Portland OR, Woburn Press, 1998).

Ignatieff, M., 'The Myth of Citizenship' in Beiner, R. (1995).

Jarolimek, J., 'The Social Studies: An Overview' in H.D. Mehlinger and O.L. Davis (eds), *The Social Studies: Eightieth Yearbook of the National Society for the Study of Education, Pt II* (Chicago IL, NSSE, 1981).

Jowell, R. and Park, A. (eds), *Young People. Politics and Citizenship: A Disengaged Generation?* (London, Citizenship Foundation, 1998).

Kant, I. *see* Reiss, H.

Kettner, J.H., *The Development of American Citizenship 1608–1870* (Chapel Hill, University of North Carolina Press, 1978).

Kohn, H., *Nationalism and Liberty: The Swiss Example* (London, Allen & Unwin, 1956).

Kymlicka, W., *Multicultural Citizenship: A Liberal Theory of Minority Rights* (Oxford, Clarendon Press, 1995).

Laursen, F., *Federalism and World Order: Compendiums I and II* (Copenhagen, World Federalist Youth, 1970/1972).

Lipsius, J. (ed. R. Kirk, trans. J. Stradling), *Two Bookes of Constancie* (New Brunswick, NJ, Rutgers University Press, 1939).

Lipson, E., *The Economic History of England. Vol. 1: The Middle Ages* (London: A. & C. Black, 13th edn, 1956),

Lister, R., *Citizenship: Feminist Perspectives* (Basingstoke, Macmillan, 1997).

Lloyd-Jones, H. (ed.), *The Greek World* (Harmondsworth, Penguin, 1965).

Locke, J., *Two Treatises of Civil Government* (London, Dent, 1962).

Macartney, C.A., *National States and National Minorities* (London, Oxford University Press, 1934).

Machiavelli, N. (ed. B. Crick), *The Discourses* (Harmondsworth, Penguin, 1998).

Marcus Aurelius Antoninus (trans. C.R. Haines), *The Communings with Himself* [i.e. *Meditations*] (London, Heinemann and Cambridge, MA, Harvard University Press, 1961).

Marshall, T.H. and Bottomore, T., *Citizenship and Social Class* (London and Concord, MA, Pluto Press, 1992).

Mátrai, Z., 'Citizenship Education in Hungary: Ideals and Reality' in Ichilov, O. (1998).

Mazzini, J., *The Duties of Man and Other Essays* (London, Dent, 1961).

Meehan, E., *Citizenship and the European Community* (London, Sage, 1993).

Merriam, C.E. (ed. and intro. G.Z.F. Bereday), *Charles E. Merriam's The Making of Citizens* (New York, Teachers College Press, Columbia University, 1966).

Meyenberg, R., 'Political Socialization of Juveniles and Political Education in Schools in the Federal Republic of Germany' in Claussen, B. and Mueller, H. (1990).

Mill, J.S., *Utilitarianism, On Liberty, and Considerations on Representative Government* (London, Dent, 1910).

Mill, J.S. (ed. and intro. S. Coit), *The Subjection of Women* (London, Longman, Green & Co., 1911).

Montesquieu, Baron de (trans. T. Nugent), *The Spirit of the Laws* (New York, Hafner, 1949).

Morison, S.E. (ed.), *Sources and Documents Illustrating the American Revolution 1764–1788* (Oxford, Clarendon Press, 2nd edn, 1929)

Oldfield, C. (ed.), *Citizenship and Community: Civic Republicanism and the Modern World* (London, Routledge, 1990).

Oommen, T.K., *Citizenship, Nationality and Ethnicity* (Cambridge, Polity Press, 1997).

Palmer, R.R., 'The National Idea in France before the Revolution' *Journal of the History of Ideas*, Vol. 1 (1940)

Palmer, R.R., *The Age of the Democratic Revolution, Vol. 1* (Princeton NJ, Princeton University Press and Oxford, Oxford University Press, 1959).

Parry, G., 'Conclusion: Paths to Citizenship' in U. Vogel and M. Moran (eds), *The Frontiers of Citizenship* (Basingstoke, Macmillan, 1991).

Plato (trans. F.M. Cornford), *The Republic of Plato* (Oxford, Clarendon Press, 1941).

Plato (trans. T.J. Saunders), *Laws* (Harmondsworth, Penguin, 1970).

Plutarch (trans. F.C. Babbitt), *Moralia,* Vol. IV (London, Heinemann, 1957).

Plutarch (trans. and intro. R.J.A. Talbert), *Plutarch on Sparta* (Harmondsworth, Penguin, 1988).

Pocock, J.G.A., 'The Ideal of Citizenship Since Classical Times' in Beiner, R. (1995).

Polenberg, R., *One Nation Divisible: Class, Race, and Ethnicity in the United States since 1938* (Harmondsworth, Penguin and New York, Viking Press, 1980).

Reiss, H. (ed.), *Kant: Political Writings* (Cambridge, Cambridge University Press, 1991).

Riesenberg, P., *Citizenship in the Western Tradition: Plato to Rousseau* (Chapel Hill, NC and London, University of North Carolina Press, 1992).

Rousseau, J.-J. (trans. B. Foxley), *Émile* (London, Dent, 1911).

Rousseau, J.-J. (trans. J.M. Cohen), *The Confessions of Jean-Jacques Rousseau* (Harmondsworth, Penguin, 1993).

Rousseau, J.-J. (trans. and intro. M. Cranston), *The Social Contract* (Harmondsworth, Penguin, 1968).

Rudé, G., *Robespierre* (London, Collins, 1975).

Schevill, F., *The Medici* (New York, Harper & Row, 1960).

Sherwin-White, A.N. , *The Roman Citizenship* (Oxford, Clarendon Press, 1973) 2nd edn.

Sieyès, E.J. (trans. M. Blondel), *What is the Third Estate?* (London, Pall Mall, 1963).

Snyder, L.L., *The Idea of Racialism* (New York, Van Nostrand, 1962).

Thomson, D., *Democracy in France: The Third and Fourth Republics* (London, RIIA/Oxford University Press, 1958).

Thompson, J.M. (ed.), *French Revolution Documents* (Oxford, Blackwell, 1948).

Thucydides (trans. R. Warner), *The Peloponnesian War* (Harmondsworth, Penguin, 1954).

Tocqueville, A. de (trans. S. Gilbert), *The Old Régime and the French Revolution* (Garden City, NY, Doubleday, 1955).

Ullmann, W., *A History of Political Thought: The Middle Ages* (Harmondsworth, Penguin, 1965).

Waley, D., *The Italian City-Republics* (London, Longman, 1988).

Walker, B. (ed.), *Uniting the Peoples and Nations* (Washington DC and Amsterdam, World Federalist Movement and World Federalist Association, 1993).

Walzer, M., 'Citizenship' in Ball, T. and Farr, J. (eds), *Political Innovation and Conceptual Change* (Cambridge, Cambridge University Press, 1989).

West, R., *Black Lamb and Grey Falcon: A Journey through Yugoslavia* (New York, Viking Press, 1963).

Wilds, E.H. and Lottich, K.V. (eds), *The Foundations of Modern Education* (New York, Holt, Rinehart and Winston, 3rd edn, 1970)

Wollstonecraft, M. (ed. M.B. Kramnick), *Vindication of the Rights of Woman* (Harmondsworth, Penguin, 1975).

Wootton, D., *Divine Right and Democracy* (Harmondsworth, Penguin, 1986).

van Steenbergen, B. (ed.), *The Condition of Citizenship* (London, Sage, 1994).

Index

CPSIA information can be obtained
at www.ICGtesting.com
Printed in the USA
JSHW042024100821
17744JS00007B/203